Before Time
Could Change Them

Before Time Could Change Them

THE COMPLETE POEMS OF

CONSTANTINE P. CAVAFY

Translated, with an Introduction and Notes, by

Theoharis Constantine Theoharis

HARCOURT, INC.

New York   San Diego   London

www.harcourt.com

Library of Congress Cataloging-in-Publication Data
Cavafy, Constantine, 1863–1933.
[Works. English. 2001]
Before time could change them: the complete poems of Constantine P. Cavafy; translated with an introduction and notes by Theoharis Constantine Theoharis. Foreword by Gore Vidal.
p.   cm.
ISBN 0-15-100519-2
1. Cavafy, Constantine, 1863–1933—Translations into English.
I. Theoharis, Theoharis Constantine.   II. Title.
PA5610.K2 A28 2001
889'.132—dc21   00-050569

Text set in Janson Text
Designed by Camilla Filancia

First edition
K J I H G F E D C B A

Printed in the United States of America

These translations are for

CHRISTOPHER SETON ABELE,

in admiration and gratitude.

ACKNOWLEDGMENTS

For their encouragement, counsel, and expertise bestowed on this project I am grateful to André Bernard, Frank Bidart, Michaelis Boutaris, Anne Fadiman, Louise Glück, Seamus Heaney, Andrew Lear, Joseph Lease, Robert Pinsky, Lloyd Schwartz, Dennis Skiotis, Tom Sleigh, Stephen Smith, and Charles M. Stang.

Contents

Foreword

Forty years ago, in a more-than-usually-rundown quarter of Athens, there was a bar called the Nea Zoe. The brightly lit raw-wood interior smelled of pine cones and licorice—retsina and ouzo. A jukebox played Greek music—minor key with a strong martial beat—to which soldiers from a nearby barracks gravely danced with one another or in groups, or alone. Women were not encouraged to join in. The Nea Zoe was a sanctuary where Greek men performed pre-Christian dances taught them by their fathers, who in turn had learned them from their fathers, and so on all the way back to the start of history, if not before. The dances celebrated the deeds of gods and heroes. I recall one astonishing—dizzying—solo in which a soldier arrived on the dance floor with a great leap and then began a series of rapid turns made while striking the floor with the flat of his hand.

"He is doing the dance of Antaeus," said the old Greek colonel who had brought me to the bar. "Antaeus was son of the sea god Poseidon, out of Gaia, Mother Earth. Antaeus is the world's strongest wrestler, but he can only remain strong by touching earth, his mother." The colonel knew all the ancient dances, and he could tell from the way a boy danced where he came from: the islands, the Peloponnese, Thessaly. "There used to be a dozen of these places here in Athens, but since that movie..." The colonel sighed. "That" movie was the recently released *Never on Sunday*; it had charmed the world, but it had also inspired many American tourists to come to places like the Nea Zoe to laugh at the dancing fairies. Since ancient Greek has no word for such a made-up category as fairy, the soldiers were at first bewildered by so much weird attention. Then, when they realized how insulting the fat Americans were, they would gravely take them outside and beat them up. Unfortunately, tourism is more important to governments than two-thousand-year–old dances; the bars were shut down.

Nea Zoe means "new life." That was also the name of the magazine where Cavafy published many of his best poems. I should note that my first visit to Athens took place in 1961, the year that *The Complete Poems of C. P. Cavafy* was published by the Hogarth Press, with an introduction by W. H. Auden. We were all reading Cavafy that season, in Rae Dalven's translation from the Greek. Now, forty years on, Theoharis Constantine Theoharis has given us what is, at last, all the poems that he could find.

Constantine P. Cavafy was born in Alexandria, April 17, 1863, not too long after Walt Whitman added "Calamus" to *Leaves of Grass.* For several generations the Cavafys were successful manufacturers and exporters. But by the time of the death of Cavafy's father, there was almost no money left. After a time in London, the widow Cavafy and six sons returned to Alexandria, in Egypt. Although Cavafy's formal education was classical, he was a bookish young man who largely educated himself while being supported by a family network until, on March 1, 1892, not quite twenty-nine—a shadow line for the young men he writes of in his poems—he became a provisional clerk in the Ministry of Irrigation. Since he had chosen to be a Greek citizen, he remained for thirty years "provisional," a permanently temporary clerk of the Egyptian government. Thanks to his knowledge of English, French, Italian, Greek, and Arabic, he sometimes moonlighted as a broker. In 1895, he acquired a civilized friend, Pericles Anastasiades, who would be for him the "other self" that Étienne de la Boétie had been for Montaigne. This was also the year Cavafy began to write "seriously." By 1903, he was being published in the Athenian magazine *Panatheneum*. A year later he published his first book, containing fourteen poems; he was now forty-one. From 1908 to 1918, he published frequently in *Nea Zoe*; he became known throughout the Greek world. Then came translations in English, French, Italian. From 1908 to 1933—the year of his death—Cavafy lived alone at 10 Lepsius Street, Alexandria, today a modest shrine. There is a long hallway lined with books and a living room that contains a large sofa and what is described as "Arab furniture"; his study was also his bedroom.

E. M. Forster famously described him at the time of the First World War:

> A Greek gentleman in a straw hat, standing absolutely motionless at a slight angle to the universe. His arms are extended, possibly. "Oh, Cavafy...!" Yes, it is Mr. Cavafy, and he is going either from his flat to the office, or from his office to the flat. If the former, he vanishes when seen, with a slight gesture of despair. If the latter, he may be prevailed upon to begin a sentence—an immense complicated yet shapely sentence, full of parentheses that never get mixed and of reservations that really do reserve; a sentence that moves with logic to its foreseen end, yet to an end that is always more vivid and thrilling than one foresaw. And despite its intellectual richness and human outlook, despite the matured charity of its judgments, one feels that it too stands at a slight angle to the universe.

Although Cavafy himself appears to have been a conventional Greek Orthodox Christian, his poetry inhabits the pagan Greco-Roman world of legend, as well as the everyday world of Alexandria in which he might be called the Pindar of the one-night stand between males. A troubled, sometime Christian, even puritan, Auden suspected that the passionate encounters Cavafy describes are largely one-sided because the poet no doubt paid for them. Although it is true that the grave soldiers at the Nea Zoe expected a small payment for their company, the business transacted was always mutual and the double nimbus of accomplished lust can be spectacularly bright in a shadowy room full of Arabian furniture, not to mention ghosts and even gods.

Yes, the gods themselves, always youthful, eternal, still appear to men:

> When an August morning dawns over you,
> your scented space gleams with their life;
> and sometimes a young man's ethereal form,
> vanishing, passing quickly, crosses the tops of your hills.

In "One of Their Gods," Cavafy observes:

> When one of them passed through Selefkia's market,
> at the hour when darkness first comes on,
> as would a tall and consummately handsome youth
> with the joy of invulnerability in his eyes...
> headed for the quarter that only lives
> at night, with orgies and debauchery,
> with every type of frenzy and abandon,
> they speculated about which of Them he was,
> and for which of his suspicious entertainments
> he'd descended to the streets of Selefkia
> from his Worshiped, his Most Venerated Halls.

Here is a standard exercise given students in classical times: Imagine that you are Julius Caesar; you have just crossed the River Rubicon; you are at war with your own republic. Now, as Caesar, write what you are thinking and feeling. A canny exercise, because to put yourself in the place of another encourages empathy and understanding. J. G. Herder even invented the German word *Einfühlen* to describe those, like Cavafy, who have the capacity to enter and inhabit other times. Some of his best poems are soliloquies that he invents for those who once lived and died in history or, more intimately, for those whom he has known and loved in his own story.

The history that he most draws upon is the world of Alexander the Great whose heirs created Greek kingdoms in Egypt and Asia Minor, sovereignties that, in less than three centuries, became powerless Roman dependencies. Marc Antony's loss of the Roman world to Octavian Augustus particularly fascinates the poet:

> Suddenly, at midnight, when an invisible troupe
> is heard passing,
> with exquisite players, with voices—
> do not lament your luck, now utterly exhausted,
> your acts that failed...
> listen, taking your final pleasure,
> to the sounds, to that mystic troupe's rare playing,

and say your last farewell to her, to that Alexandria you are
losing.

For Cavafy, Alexandria, not Cleopatra, is the heroine of the
hero's tragedy.

Despite Cavafy's sense that the old gods have never forsaken
us, he shows no sympathy at all for the Emperor Julian who, vainly,
tried to restore the worship of the gods in the fourth century.
Admittedly, Julian could be a grinding bore but, even so, the essen-
tially pagan Cavafy should have admired him. But he doesn't. Why
not? I think one pronoun shows us what Cavafy is up to: "In Anti-
och we were perplexed on hearing / about Julian's latest behavior."
There it is. *We.* Cavafy is writing as a Christian citizen of Antioch, a
city that disdained the emperor and all his works. *Einfühlen* at work.
Cavafy is like an actor here, in character—or like Shakespeare when
he imagines himself nephew to a murdered king even though, ac-
cording to one of Cavafy's most ingenious poems, it is Claudius who
is the good king and Hamlet, the student prince, the villain. The
youth "was nervous in the extreme. / While he was studying in Wit-
tenberg / many of his fellow students thought him a maniac."

Cavafy once analyzed his own temperament and talent: "To me,
the immediate impression is never a starting point for work. The im-
pression has got to age, has got to falsify itself with time, without my
having to falsify it.

"I have two capacities: to write Poetry or to write History. I
haven't written History and it's too late now. Now, you'll say, how do
I know that I could write History? I feel it. I make the experiment,
and ask myself: Cavafy, could you write fiction? Ten voices cry No. I
ask the question again: Cavafy, could you write a play? Twenty-five
voices again cry No. Then I ask again: Cavafy, could you write His-
tory? A hundred and twenty-five voices tell me you could." The
critic Robert Liddell thought Cavafy could have been a master of
historical fiction. Luckily, he chose to be himself, a unique poet at an
odd angle to our culture.

It was noted at the death of America's tragic twentieth-century
empress—the one who died with a Greek name as well as fate—that

her favorite poem was Cavafy's "Ithaca." One can see why. Cavafy has gone back to Homer: to the origin of Greek narrative. Odysseus, returning from Troy to his home island of Ithaca, is endlessly delayed by the malice of the sea god Poseidon. Cavafy appears to be addressing Odysseus himself, but it could be anyone on a life's journey: "As you set out toward Ithaca, / hope the way is long, / full of reversals, full of knowing." He advises the traveler not to brood too much on the malice of those who want to destroy him, to keep him from his goal. *If you don't take them to heart, they cannot defeat you.* The poet also advises the traveler to enjoy the exotic cities along the way; he even favors selective shopping, something that also appealed to our nineteenth-century tragic empress, Mrs. Abraham Lincoln. Why not take advantage of a visit to Egypt for wisdom?

> Keep Ithaca always in your mind.
> Arriving there is what has been ordained for you.
> But do not hurry the journey at all.
> Better if it lasts many years;
> and you dock an old man on the island,
> rich with all that you have gained on the way,
> not expecting Ithaca to give you wealth.
>
> Ithaca gave you the beautiful journey.
> Without her you would not have set out.
> She has nothing more to give you.

Then, the final insight, acceptance of a life now lived: "And if you find her poor, Ithaca has not fooled you. / Having become so wise, with so much experience, / you will have understood, by then, what these Ithacas mean." One does need to be a tragic empress to be impressed by Cavafy's practical wisdom.

Finally, one is in Mr. Theoharis's debt for a poem that I have never seen before. It is called "Eternity":

> The Indian king Arjuna, humane and mild,
> hated slaughter. He never waged war.

But the fearful war god was displeased—

. . .

and in a mighty rage he entered the palace of Arjuna.
The king was afraid and said: "Great God,
forgive me if I cannot take a human life!"
With contempt the god answered: "You think
yourself more just than I? Don't be fooled by words.
Not one life is taken. Know that no one
was ever born, nor does anyone die."

This is, suddenly, in the midst of the turbulent Greco-Roman
world, the calm voice of Krishna. All is illusion for the enlightened.
Plainly, Cavafy, himself no Arjuna, did achieve something very like
that ultimate state of enlightenment where, not fooled by words, he
was able to so order them as to make our common voyage, viewed
from his unique angle, seem beautiful, even consoling, in its shining
nothingness.

GORE VIDAL

Introduction

Let All Its Guarded Passion Shine

Eros and civilization never entirely command or obey the natural forces in which they arise. The soul longs for perfected, energetic rest in the beloved; the citizen aspires to excellent accomplishments in worldly life, while the beloved keeps somehow always withdrawn and the world toys with all excellent achievements. Lyric poetry, history, and moral philosophy bear witness to this longing and aspiration, now celebrating the pursuit, now staying losses. These three modes of writing, which Cavafy himself applied as descriptive categories to his work, all center on passion, the willed engagement with contingency, and all protect and check, all guard, the soul and citizen who lives toward and from that center. The permitting-and-denying limit on passion in Cavafy's poems shines variously as irony, nostalgia, stoical reserve, and yielding tenderness. Sage and sophisticate, Cavafy the lover, the historian, and the moralist shows how beauty shines at the limit of human striving, and reveals what the journeying soul and the man of flesh might be permitted to see in that glory.

The first view of things may very well be shabby or falsely bright for the speaker or protagonist in these poems. Memory is often called on in the poems to restore beauty's erotic force to an isolated man parted from another man he kissed ecstatically but could not keep. Poverty and the abuses that attend it assign exquisitely desirable men to early graves, to neglect, or to anonymous ruin. The opprobrium conventional morality casts on homosexuality corrupts romances, distorts longing, and puts a frightened halt to living in or even searching out the body's innocence and joy. Or, more simply and more sadly, love is trumped by work or jealousy or death.

In all these erotic losses, Cavafy preserves the refined fulfillment that charges the rare poems of perfected eros that he wrote: Rapture abides at the limit passion sets on bodies. Homosexuality may set those limits more severely—and Cavafy is rightly prized for the frankness and courage he showed in testing them—but it does not set them uniquely. However it appears, passion brings the soul a shining guard.

To some extent an anachronism in the late nineteenth and early twentieth centuries Cavafy lived and wrote in, the term *soul* is the ground of thought and feeling in the period and place in which Cavafy sets the bulk of his historical poems: late antiquity in the Hellenistic urban centers of the Mediterranean and of Asia Minor—Alexandria, Antioch, Beirut; capitals of Alexander's empire that were gradually absorbed into Rome's by the fourth century C.E. Platonic, Neoplatonic, Hebraic, Christian, and Stoic thought and writing jostle in this period together with ascending and descending empires—Macedonian Alexander's, Roman Octavian's, those of Egypt's Ptolemaic and Persia's Seleucid dynastic families—for governance of the soul and its worldly circumstances.

Cavafy's historical figures negotiate these competing authorities in the borrowed light of exile, quixotic rebellion, elegant dissipation, and tragic renunciation. A leading figure in the diaspora Greek civilization of Alexandria while it was governed by the modern British Empire, Cavafy transferred the shabby gentility of his own personal circumstances (his financially declined family descended, on his mother's side, from the Phanar, the once elite Greek district of modern Constantinople) and the guarded marginality of his contemporary political and economic status (he worked until middle age as a clerk in Alexandria's waterworks bureau and then lived from market speculation) to his Hellenistic protagonists. These include nomadic men of letters, sophists, scholars, and their followers and pupils; musicians, sculptors, and their patrons; puppet monarchs; ousted courtiers; financial and sexual adventurers; variously authentic Greek Orthodox laity and clergy; and a far-flung fraternity of political intriguers made up of usurped and usurping rulers, mercenaries, propagandists, and bureaucrats. For all these men, and occasional women, history is a challenge: Master a mastering force, preserve what has been received even as it vanishes. Those who fail the challenge, through venality, vainglory, cowardice, or nihilistic weariness, Cavafy treats with acid sarcasm or genial disdain. Those who take up the challenge successfully, not by winning what the world offers but by comporting themselves in the world beautifully and justly, by guarding their intellects and imaginations against power's blandishments, and time's, Cavafy preserves in poems of elemental dignity: honorific encapsulated lives that transform in miniature the classical form perfected by Plutarch; or dramatic monologues, usually tragic utterances that extend the mysteriously admirable presentation of character offered in Browning and Shakespeare.

While Cavafy moralizes often in his love poems and history poems, he also presents the soul seeking equipoise alone, in poems best understood as spiritual exercises, didactic confrontations with limit thought of as an agonistic force the soul can master rather than a circumstance it is merely fated to endure. These monologues of counsel make endurance a tactic the wise soul can command to serve the strategic end of living with the given as a resource for self-creation. That strategy guards and magnifies the soul, especially when what is given disappoints. In these spiritual exercises Cavafy advances the late classical and early Christian insight according to which the soul ambiguously orders and is ordered by the promises of well-being ceaselessly proffered and withdrawn by beauty and justice. The ascetic sensuality of Epicureanism and the ascetic joy of Christian aspiration coalesce in Cavafy's wisdom poems, urging on the soul openness to erotic life and disciplined engagement in humanistic accomplishment. More radically, these poems also require the soul to take the encountered limits that exalt as well as inevitably constrict it in these spheres, and convert them to limits that it soberly, and, at the height of its tested powers, blissfully bestows.

What force, what discipline or bliss renders a discovered limit an order that the soul bestows? Cavafy's answer makes no use of the modernists' ungrounded Will, the supreme man's heroically personal command, "I will have it thus," but draws instead on pagan and Christian Hellenism, on the primacy that a world of thought and feeling placed on the soul's essential function: active reception of contingency, the refining pursuit of energetic rest in imperfectly presented havens. The soul attains this equipoise, half actual, half fashioned in the mind, through aesthetic contemplation of beauty at its limit and through aristocratic demeanor, a self-proclaiming but not self-seeking presence to power at its limit. Limited conditions call forth transformation in the soul, activate its power to move through one given form of experience to another. That motion changes not only the moving soul but also the form that the soul passes through, and it is in this dual change that a testing discovery of limit becomes a bestowal of that same limit, one the soul makes with discipline and bliss.

United with the beautiful form of any body, the soul and that form coalesce in an energetic rest that endures sublimely at the limit where the union occurred. Erotic loss stays loss when the body vanishes, but the aesthetic apprehension of the beautiful form that eros sublimely called forth in the soul also stays loss, holds it off by retaining the cherished form within the soul. Hence the premium on beauty and artistic responsiveness and creativity in Cavafy's poems, themselves disciplined by exquisite standards of formal integrity, blissful in cherished apprehension. United with the dignifying form of justice in its self-presentation to power, the soul and that ideal form of conduct similarly coalesce. Worldly loss stays loss for the balked aristocratic soul in the same dual way. Hence the premium on magnanimity in Cavafy's poems, a spiritual largesse soberly disciplined by unfailing ethical integrity, blissful in its self-preservation from all dependence on worldly recompense. At external limits the soul's interior forces rise; in wise souls the guarded transformation that the crisis calls forth irradiates the limit and the soul together in one beam, the energetic rest that Cavafy made poetry's origin and end.

The coarsest grappling with limits—ridicule—Cavafy normally avoids, but he deploys the midrange of refined contest with inadequate experience—irony—regularly and masterfully. Whimsically forbearing, poignantly aloof, or reservedly empathic, the ironic poems focus on what *cannot* be transformed in limited conditions. At times the speakers of these poems dispense the irony courageously or languidly, admirably aware of what they can and cannot save for the soul from some folly it has encountered. At times the poems play ironically past the speakers directly to the reader, presenting folly's ruin as a passing show to be grimly marveled at or indulgently shunned by those who have passed through but have not fallen victim to the innumerable and efflorescent forms of decadence that battle to possess the soul. Without the prophet's savage indignation or the reformer's zeal, Cavafy's irony turns a many-minded and therefore liberating gaze on calcified appearances, sporting elegantly when it encounters camouflage, laughing bravely when it comes to rest in any challenge made by truth.

Poetry works the known and felt values of thought and feeling into language that formal compression has essentially made into music. The devices for such compression abound—metaphor, simile, image, symbol, varieties in verse form and in genre, and their penetration through and by the combinatory wealth of rhythm, rhyme, and assonance. Cavafy's compression results more in nuanced, rather than faceted, complexity. He almost never structures poems symbolically after his earliest work, and he rarely uses metaphors, relying more on similes and images. These routinely appear as elements in the direct statement of an idea or in the expression of a feeling in his poems, rather than as isolated or enigmatically arranged correlative structures that render thoughts or sensations as emotions. As his career progressed he rhymed less and less strictly, preferring internal assonance and ambient end-rhymes to regularly patterned repetition. His rhythms likewise moved less rigidly in the middle and later work, which takes its shape mostly from long paragraphs through which a few sentences turn slowly, organized more by the spontaneity of speech than by grammatical or thematic abstraction. More than any other modern Greek poet, Cavafy bypassed rhetoric, figurative and ornamental speech, working instead primarily and elementally with diction and syntax. The right words in the right order are, in Cavafy's case, minimally formal elements of common speech made maximally efficient in sequences that hover at the open limit between conversational spontaneity and compositional rigor. Faceted complexity keeps poetry wondrously abstract; nuanced complexity keeps poetry enigmatically open. Finally, for all his interiority, Cavafy is essentially a poet of what's open, of what joy there is to be caught up in and to affirm when the soul and the world hover together at the limit of spontaneity and rigor.

A NOTE ON TRANSLATING CAVAFY

Translation has much to do with faith, as defined by St. Paul in a letter to the Hebrews (Heb. 11:1); it, too, is "the substance of things hoped for, the evidence of things not seen." In poetic translation the object of the translator's and audience's faith is the music a foreign language gives to experience, and in Cavafy's poems that music is essentially a tone of voice, an emotional and intellectual disposition imbuing the meters, rhymes, and verse forms in which he worked. Because he wrote extensively in iambics, Cavafy's meter has not been difficult to match in English. His verse forms are likewise little marred by this transposition. His rhymes cannot be carried over; nor can his assonance. Readers avid for access to the meanings these make in Cavafy's poems are invited here to cross over into the new life that knowledge of modern Greek bestows. A brief description of the nature of that language is included in this volume's note for "To Jerusalem."

I have worked to bring Cavafy's tone of voice into a new English key here, primarily to render his decorous intensity, and to convey the urbane clarity of his learned engagement with elemental experience. I have kept the same number of lines in each translation as appear in the original Greek poem and, whenever possible, maintained Cavafy's line and paragraph breaks. And, with the exceptions listed below, I have kept Cavafy's verse forms intact.

In the following poems—"The Battle of Magnesia," "Prayer," "Julian in Nicomedia," "31 B.C. in Alexandria," "A Great Feast at the Home of Sosibios"—Cavafy made rhyming couplets separate stanzas. Because I have not rhymed these poems, I have run the two-line stanzas into continuous stanzas. In the following poems—"He Swears," "In the Month of Athyr," "Craftsman of Winebowls," "Before Antiochus Epiphanis," "Desperation," "Theater of Sidon (400 A.D.)," "Before Time Could Change Them," "Temethos, Antiochian; 400 A.D.," "That They Might Appear," "Julian in Nicomedia," "On an Italian Shore," "In the Wineshops—," "Sophist Departing from Syria," "Days of 1896," "Greek from Ancient Times," "Picture of a Young Man, Twenty-three, Done by His Friend of the Same Age, an Amateur," "Kimon, Son of Learchos, Age 22, Student of Greek Literature (in Kyrini)," "Flowers White and Beautiful, as Were Most Becoming"—Cavafy split each line into two parts divided by a central spatial break that amounts to a caesura. The musical effect cannot properly be recreated in English, so I have omitted the spatial break and made the lines single, continuous units. Translators, like all writers, are, in T. S. Eliot's dictum from *East Coker*, "Trying to learn to use words . . . / . . . And . . . each venture / Is a new beginning, a raid on the inarticulate." I have learned much from the earlier forays into Cavafy's poems made by the translators Rae Dalven, Edmund Keeley and Philip Sherrard, and John Mavrogordato. For whatever in these renditions of Cavafy remains "inarticulate," and the result of "shabby equipment always deteriorating," as Eliot continues to put the problem of learning to write in *East Coker*, I ask the reader's forbearance.

A TEXTUAL NOTE

I have translated the standard texts of Cavafy's poems established by George Savidis: *Poems: Volume 1 (1897–1918), Volume II (1919–1933)*, Ikaros Press, Athens, 1991; *Hidden Poems (1877–1923)*, Ikaros Press, Athens, 1993; and *Rejected Poems*, Ikaros Press, Athens, 1983. I have not included the thirty fragments and sketches collected by R. Lavagnini in *C. P. Cavafy, Unfinished Poems 1918–1932*, Ikaros Press, Athens, 1994. Although some of his poems appeared in journals, Cavafy did not publish volumes with commercial houses. It was his habit to write seventy or so poems a year, destroy most of them, and circulate the rest in printed broadsheets to his inner circle of friends and relatives. By the end of his life, Cavafy devised three collections of his poetry: two printed booklets, entitled *Poems: 1905–1915* and *Poems: 1916–1918*, and a remaining group, made of the broadsheets excluded from the booklets and called *Poems: 1919–1932*. Cavafy arranged the booklets thematically and the uncollected broadsheets chronologically. I have adopted Cavafy's thematic sequences for the booklets here, where the poems appear for the first time in English in the reverberant order Cavafy established for them in his artistic maturity. The uncollected broadsheets appear here chronologically, as "Unpublished Poems: 1919–1932." The group here entitled "Hidden Poems" contains work Cavafy considered unfinished or otherwise unworthy of private or public circulation. I have presented these poems in the historical sequence he established for them in his own records. "Rejected Poems" contains early poems that Cavafy repudiated. They are presented here in the order of composition recorded by Cavafy.

Cavafy also translated selections from Tennyson, Keats, Shelley, Dante, and Shakespeare into Greek. I have excluded these, together with his translation from the French, "Had You Loved Me," and his poems in English, "More Happy Thou, Performing Member," "Leaving Therapia," and "Darkness and Shadow," from this collection; they can be found in Savidis's edited volume, *Hidden Poems*. The following nine works have not appeared in English collections of Cavafy's poems before: "Stephanos Skilitsis," "To Jerusalem," "A Second Odyssey," "*La Jeunesse blanche*," "The Cat," "The Regiment of Pleasure," "The Ships," "Garments," and "The Footsteps of the Eumenides."

POEMS: 1905–1915

The City

You said: "I will go to another land, I will go to another sea.
Another city will turn up, a better one than this.
My efforts—each is judged and damned beforehand,
and my heart is buried, like a dead man.
And my mind, how long will it remain in this morass.
Anywhere I turn my eye, anywhere I look,
the black ruins of my life are what I see here,
where I have spent so many years, where I have botched and spoiled
    so many."

You will not find other places, you will not find other seas.
The city will follow you. All roads you walk
will be these roads. And you will age in these same neighborhoods;
and in these same houses you will go gray.
Always you will end up in this city. For you
there is no boat—abandon hope of that—no road to other things.
The way you've botched your life here, in this small corner,
makes for your ruin everywhere on earth.

The Satrapy

What a calamity, given how ready you are
for fine, distinguished tasks,
that this unjust fate of yours
always denies you encouragement and success;
that mean habits block you,
both pettiness and indifference.
And how horrible the day you give way
(the day you allow it all and give way)
and tramp off to Susa,
and go to King Artaxerxes,
who places you, favorably, in his court,
who makes you gifts of satrapies and such.
And you accept them with despair,
those situations which you do not want.
Your soul demands other things, cries for them;
commendation from the city's Rulers and the Sophists,
contested, priceless, clamorous Approval—
the Agora, the Theater, and the Laurels.
How can Artaxerxes give you these,
where will you find these in the satrapy,
and what life will you lead without them.

The Wise Sense Imminent Events

Gods perceive future events, mortals present ones, whereas the wise
sense those that are imminent.
    —Philostratos, *Life of Apollonios of Tyana* VIII

Mortals know present events.
The gods know those in the future,
sole and full presiders over all the light.
Of what is to come the wise notice
what is imminent. Their hearing,

now and then, in times of somber study,
is violently disrupted. The secret roar
of things approaching comes to them.
And they give it reverent attention. Whereas outdoors
in the road, the common sort hear nothing whatsoever.

The Ides of March

Oh soul, fear things grandiose.
And if you are unable to master your ambitions,
serve them with hesitation, with precaution.
And the farther you advance,
the more you must be questioning and careful.

And when you reach your height, Caesar finally;
when you take up the form of a man that renowned,
then take great care as you go out into the street,
the striking dignitary with an entourage,
if it happens that from the crowd
a certain Artemidoros comes near, who brings a letter,
and rushed says "Read this immediately,
it speaks of grave matters that concern you,"
don't miss the opportunity to stop; to put off
all talk, every task; don't miss the chance
to cast off those random praisers and scrapers
(you can see them later); let even the Senate itself wait
for this, and learn at once
what gravity is in the writing of Artemidoros.

Things Run Out

Amid fear and suspicions,
with a shocked mind and frightened eyes,
we break down and scheme to find out
how we might escape that certain danger
threatening us with so much horror.
But we are mistaken, that end's not on the way:
the signals were false
(or we didn't hear or understand them properly).
Another doom, which we had not imagined,
sudden, headlong falls on us,
and carries us—not ready, with no time left—utterly away.

The God Forsakes Antony

Suddenly, at midnight, when an invisible troupe
is heard passing,
with exquisite players, with voices—
do not lament your luck, now utterly exhausted,
your acts that failed, your life's projects,
all ended in delusion.
Like a man who's all along been ready, like a man made bold by it,
say your last farewell to her, to Alexandria, who is leaving.
First, foremost, do not fool yourself,
and say it was a dream, or that your ears were tricked;
do not stoop to such vacant hopes.
Like a man who's all along been ready, like a man made bold by it,
in a way fitting the dignity that made you worthy of such a city,
approach the window steadily,
and listen, moved, but not needy
and disgruntled, like a coward,
listen, taking your final pleasure,
to the sounds, to that mystic troupe's rare playing,
and say your last farewell to her, to that Alexandria you are losing.

Theodotos

If you are one of the truly elect,
be careful of how you acquire your mastering force.
However much you are glorified, however much
the cities proclaim your exploits
in Italy and Thessaly,
however many honorific votes you win
from those who marvel at you in Rome,
neither your happiness, nor your triumph will endure,
nor will you feel exalted—how exalted?—
when, in Alexandria, Theodotos brings you,
on a bloodied salver,
wretched Pompey's head.

And do not rest content that your life,
confined, settled, pedestrian,
does not admit such spectacular, such fearsome things.
Perhaps at this hour, into a well-kept
neighbor's house—unseen, bodiless—
Theodotos enters,
bearing exactly such a freakish head.

Monotony

One monotonous day follows
another monotonous one identically.
The same things will happen and happen again—
the same moments find and leave us.

A month goes by and brings another month.
The things to come one readily surmises:
those boring on the previous day.
And tomorrow, reduced so, no longer seems tomorrow.

Ithaca

As you set out toward Ithaca,
hope the way is long,
full of reversals, full of knowing.
Laistrygonians and Cyclops,
angry Poseidon you should not fear,
never will you find such things on your way
if your thought stays lofty, if refined
emotion touches your spirit and your body.
Laistrygonians and Cyclops,
savage Poseidon you will not meet,
if you do not carry them with you in your soul,
if your soul does not raise them up before you.

Hope the way is long.
May there be many summer mornings when,
with what pleasure, with what joy,
you shall enter first-seen harbors;
may you stop at Phoenician bazaars
and acquire the fine things sold there,
nacre and coral, amber and ebony,
and sensual perfumes, every kind there is,
as much as you can abundant sensual perfumes;
may you go to many Egyptian cities
to learn and learn again from those educated.

Keep Ithaca always in your mind.
Arriving there is what has been ordained for you.
But do not hurry the journey at all.
Better if it lasts many years;
and you dock an old man on the island,
rich with all that you've gained on the way,
not expecting Ithaca to give you wealth.

Ithaca gave you the beautiful journey.
Without her you would not have set out.
She has nothing more to give you.

And if you find her poor, Ithaca has not fooled you.
Having become so wise, with so much experience,
you will have understood, by then, what these Ithacas mean.

As Long as You Can

And even if you cannot make your life what you want,
for as long as you can, at least
try to do this: do not trivialize it
in all the busy contacts of the world,
in all the swarm and gossip.

Do not trivialize it, hauling it,
roaming with it, always exposing it
to the pairings and relations
of everyday stupidity,
until it ends up irritating, stubborn as a beggar.

Trojans

Our efforts are those of men caught in calamity;
our efforts are like those of the Trojans.
We accomplish a little, we pretend
to a little more power, and we start
trusting our courage and great expectations.

But always something emerges and stops us.
Achilles appears from the trench before us
and appalls us with haughty shouting.—

Our efforts are like those of the Trojans.
We imagine that with decision and audacity
we will change the blow fate deals us,
and out we stand for combat.

But when the major crisis comes,
our decision and audacity desert us;
our soul is shocked, it trembles, paralytic;
and circling the walls we run
looking for our safety in our flight.

But our fall is certain. Overhead,
on the walls, the lamentation already has begun.
Memories of our days, of their shared grace, are wept for.
Bitterly for us Priam and Hecuba are weeping.

King Dimitrios

As if he were not a king, but an actor,
he disguised himself with a gray mantle
in exchange for his tragic one,
and escaping notice departed.
    —Plutarch, *Life of Dimitrios*

When the Macedonians forsook him
and so proved they valued Pyrrhus more,
King Dimitrios (possessing
a great soul) behaved—so they said—
in no way like a king. Straightaway
he took off his golden robes,
and cast aside his purple,
knee-laced boots. He dressed
in simple clothes, quickly, and left unobserved.
He did exactly what an actor would
who, when the performance ends,
changes what he wears and takes his leave.

The Glory of the Ptolemies

I am Lagides, king. In perfect possession
(by my power and my wealth) of pleasure.
Not a Macedonian or barbarian can be found
who equals me or in any way comes close. Selefkos's
son, commonly debauched, is laughable.
If, however, you seek to know more, behold all this as well.
The city instructing all others, the Panhellenic summit,
in every kind of learning, in every kind of art, more wise than any.

Procession of Dionysus

Damon the artisan (in all the Peloponnese
there's no one more skilled), working
Parian marble, perfects each final grace
in the procession of Dionysus. The god leads
with divine glory, with power in his steps.
Intemperance follows. At the side of Intemperance
Drunkenness pours wine to the Satyrs
from an amphora crowned with ivy.
Near him cosseted Honeywine,
his eyes half-shut, drifting asleep.
And farther behind come the singers
Molpos and Sweet Tune, with Comus who
never allows the revered torch of the march,
which he holds, to go out; and also, most modestly, Ritual.—
These Damon shapes. And his mind
fastens now and then on a closely
related topic, his wages from the Syracusans' king:
three talents, a grand amount.
With the money he already has, and this new sum coming in soon,
he can live as an eminent, prosperous man,
he can become a politician—the joy of it!—
he too in the Senate, he too in the Agora.

The Battle of Magnesia

He's lost his old daring, his nerve.
His weary body will be his chief care soon.
And what remains of his life he'll manage unconcerned.
That, at least, is what Philip asserts.
Tonight he's tossing dice; he's eager to enjoy himself.
Put a lot of roses on the table. What if
Antiochus was destroyed at Magnesia? They say
his massed and splendid troops suffered heavy losses.
It's possible they've exaggerated; it's not likely
all of that is true. That much can be wished.
Since, however opposed as foes, we are both one race.
Still, one such "wished" suffices. It may even be too much.
Philip will certainly not postpone the celebration.
However much exhaustion stays his life,
one benefit remains: his memory is intact. He recalls
how they wailed in Syria, what kind of grief they felt,
when their mother Macedonia was cut down to a scrap.
Let the banquet start. Slaves: the flutes, the torches.

The Displeasure of Selefkides

Dimitrios Selefkides was displeased
to learn that a Ptolemy had reached
Italy in such shameful disarray.
With only two or three slaves;
in poor clothes and on foot. They'll
be brought down this way, end up an irony;
their lineage a Roman toy. That they've basically
become Roman servants of a sort Selefkides knows,
he knows that those people
give and take away their thrones
high-handedly, however pleasure moves them.
But at least when they present themselves
they ought to keep intact some grandeur;
and this way not forget that they are kings still,
that they (alas!) are called kings still.

This is what troubled Dimitrios
Selefkides: and immediately he offered the Ptolemy
purple garments, a shining diadem,
precious jewelry, a great number
of attendants in procession, his most expensive horses,
so that he might present himself to Rome properly,
as an Alexandrian Greek monarch.

But Lagides, who had come to beg,
knew his business and refused them all:
he had no need whatsoever of these luxuries.
In threadbare clothes, he humbly entered Rome,
and found lodging at a minor craftsman's house.
And after that he presented himself
as some hard-luck case, some poor soul to the Senate,
so as to enhance his reward for begging.

Orophernis

The man on this four-drachma piece
with something like a smile on his face,
his handsome, refined face,
that man is Orophernis, son of Ariarathis.

They drove him, while a child, out of Cappadocia,
out of the grand palace of his fathers,
and sent him to grow up in Ionia,
and so to be forgotten among strangers.

Ah splendid those Ionian nights,
when fearlessly, and in consummately Greek form,
he first knew fully passion's joy.
In his heart, always Asiatic;
but in his bearing and his speech, Greek,
adorned with turquoise stones, in Greek dress,
his body laved in jasmine balm,
of all the handsome Ionian youths
the most handsome, surpassingly voluptuous.

Afterwards, when the Syrians
came into Cappadocia, and made him king,
he rushed into the monarch's role
to please himself in some new manner every day,
to amass by seizure gold and silver,
and then delight and vaunt,
seeing upheaped treasures gleam.
As for the cares of state and governing—
he was blind to everything that happened all around him.

The Cappadocians quickly ousted him;
and he wound up in Syria, at the palace of Dimitrios,
entertaining himself and idling.

One day, however, unusual reflections
interrupted his endless holiday;
he recalled that through his mother Antiochida,
and through that old grandmother Stratoniki
he too had a claim to the crown of Syria,
and was nearly a Selefkid.
For a while he turned away from lust and drunkenness,
and incompetently, dimly giddy,
sought to hatch an intrigue,
to do something, scheme somehow,
but he accomplished nothing, and finally caved in.

Somewhere his end was probably recorded and then lost;
or perhaps history came across it
and, with its justice, would not condescend
to notice so slight a matter.

The man on this four-drachma piece
left one grace from his handsome youth,
one light from his poetic beauty,
one aesthetic memory of a boy from Ionia;
that is Orophernis, son of Ariarathis.

Alexandrian Kings

The Alexandrians flocked
to view the children of Cleopatra,
Kaisarion and his little brothers,
Alexander and Ptolemy, who for the first time
had been brought out to the Gymnasium,
to be proclaimed kings there,
amidst the gleaming company of soldiers on parade.

Alexander—him they named king
of Armenia, Media, and the Parthians.
Ptolemy—him they named king
of Cilicia, Syria, and Phoenicia.
Kaisarion was standing furthest forward,
dressed in rose-toned silk,
on his breast a clutch of hyacinths,
his belt paired lines of sapphires and amethysts,
his shoes laced by white
ribbons pinned with rose-blush pearls.
Him they named higher than the younger ones,
him they named King of Kings.

The Alexandrians certainly understood
that these were words and histrionics.

But the day was warm and poetic,
the sky a clear, wide blue,
the Alexandrian Gymnasium a
triumphant artistic feat,
the courtiers luxury at its crest,
Kaisarion all grace and beauty
(the son of Cleopatra, blood of the Lagids);
and the Alexandrians raced to the festive name-day,

and worked themselves into raptures, and called out
cheers in Greek, in Egyptian, and some in Hebrew,
enchanted by the lovely spectacle—
even though they very clearly knew the value of these things,
what inane words made up these titled kings.

Philhellene

See that the engraving is done skillfully.
The expression serious and majestic.
The diadem preferably somewhat narrow:
I dislike those wide things the Parthians have.
Greek, as usual, for the inscription:
not hyperbolic, not pompous—
so that the proconsul can't mistake it while he's
scavenging for faults to send back endlessly to Rome—
but still, of course, honorific.
Something very choice for the other side:
some handsome discus-thrower in his teens.
Above all I urge you to take special care
(Sithaspis, for God's sake, this mustn't be forgotten)
that after the titles King and Savior
there be engraved, in elegant letters, Philhellene.
At this point don't start playing the sophisticate,
indulging in arch rhetoric, "Where are the Greeks?" and
"What can be Greek behind Zagros here, so far outside of Phraata?"
Since so many others more barbarous than us
inscribe it, we will inscribe it too.
And finally don't forget that on occasion
Sophists come to us from Syria,
and versifiers, and other vainly learned sorts.
I wouldn't say that we're not hellenized.

The Footsteps

In an ebony bed adorned
with coral eagles, Nero sleeps soundly—
unwitting, peaceful, happy;
in the flesh's highest force,
in the beautiful crest of youth.

But in the alabaster hall that shelters
the ancient shrine of the Aenobarbi—
how its Lares are troubled.
The little household gods tremble
and try to hide their unimportant bodies.
Because they've heard an inauspicious sound,
a deadly rumbling rising on the stairway,
iron footsteps shaking all the stairs.
And fainting now, the miserable Lares
push to hide deep in the shrine,
jostling and stumbling, one over the other,
one little god falls on top of another,
because they've understood what sort of noise this is,
they've discerned by now the footsteps of the Erinyes.

Herodis Attikos

What glory, this, for Herodis Attikos.

Alexander the Selefkian, one of our better sophists,
arriving in Athens to speak,
finds the city empty, because Herodis
was in the country. And the young men
had all followed him to listen to him there.
So the sophist Alexander writes
a letter to Herodis,
requesting that he send back the Greeks.
And the tactful Herodis replies at once,
"I'll come along as well, accompanying the Greeks."—

How many fellows now in Alexandria,
in Antioch, or in Beirut
(being trained by Hellenism as its future orators),
when they gather at the best tables,
where at times the talk is about fine sophistry,
and at times about their ecstatic loves,
are silent suddenly, preoccupied.
They leave the glasses next to them untouched,
and contemplate how fortune's favored Herodis—
what other sophist has proved worthy of such things?—
that the Greeks (the Greeks!) should follow him,
whatever he desires, whatever he does,
not to criticize him, or to debate,
not even to choose now, only to follow.

Tyanan Sculptor

As you'll have heard, I'm no beginner.
I've handled lots of stone.
And in my own country, Tyana, I'm
well known; and I've had many statues
commissioned by senators here.

                    Let me show you
a few of them now. Notice this Rhea:
reverential, all fortitude, utterly archaic.
Notice Pompey. Marius,
Paulus Aemilius, Scipio Africanus.
A faithful likeness, every one, as far as I was able.
Patroklos (I plan to work on him a little more).
Over near those slightly yellow
marble segments is Kaisarion.

And for some time now I've been busy
doing a Poseidon. His horses are my
greatest formal challenge, discovering a shape for them.
They must be done so weightlessly that
their bodies, their feet will clearly show
they're not stepping on the earth, but running over water.

But here's my favorite work,
on which I labored lovingly and with the most attention;
this one—one day in the summer's heat
when my mind rose to ideal things—
this one came as I dreamed of the young Hermes.

Tomb of the Grammarian Lysias

Directly on the right as you enter the library
in Beirut we buried wise Lysias,
the grammarian. The spot is beautifully chosen.
We put him near those things of his that he remembers
even there, perhaps—annotations, texts, analytic grammars,
variants, volumes in series interpreting idiomatic Greek.
Also, this way, as we go to the books,
his tomb will be seen and honored by us.

Tomb of Evrion

In this artfully carved sepulcher,
all of it syenite stone,
that masses of lilies and violets cover,
handsome Evrion is buried.
An Alexandrian youth, twenty-five years old.
On his father's side, old Macedonian stock;
on his mother's a long line of magistrates.
He was tutored by Aristokleitos in philosophy,
by Paros in rhetoric. At Thebes he studied
the sacred texts. He wrote a history
of the prefecture of Arsinoitos. That at least will last.
But what was most precious we've lost, his form—
that was like seeing Apollo in rapture.

That's the Man

Unknown—a stranger in Antioch—the man from Edessa
writes and writes. And at last, there,
the final canto's done. That makes eighty-three

poems in all. But so much writing
has wearied the poet, so much versifying,
so much straining to phrase things in Greek,
and now every part of it burdens him, bores him completely.

But a thought suddenly brings him
out of his funk—the exalting That's the Man
which formerly Lucian heard in his sleep.

Dangerous Remarks

Said Myrtias (a Syrian student
in Alexandria; during the reign
of Konstantinos Augustus and Konstantinios Augustus;
in part a pagan, and in part a Christian convert):
"Made strong in thought and contemplation,
I will not, like some coward, fear my passions.
My body I will give to pleasures,
and to those dreamed-of joys,
to longings where eros is most brazen,
to everything aroused and surging in my blood, without
one fear, because when I want to—
and I'll have the will, made strong
by then in thought and contemplation—
at the decisive moments I shall once more
find my soul, as it was before, ascetic."

Manuel Komninos

The Emperor Manuel Komninos
one melancholy day in September
felt death at hand. The court astrologers
(who had been paid) chattered
that he would live on for many more years.
But in the midst of their talk, he
remembers the old reverend customs,
and from the cells of the eremites orders
ecclesiastical robes to be brought,
and he wears them, exulting in the
appearance he gives of a modest priest or monk.

Happy all those who believe,
and like the Emperor Manuel end things
dressed modestly in their faith.

In Church

I love the church—its standards bearing cherubim,
the altar's silver articles, the candlesticks,
the lights, its icons, its pulpits.

When I step inside there, into a church of the Greeks;
with its incense aromas,
with its liturgical voices and harmonies,
the attendant priests majestic,
their movements all a solemn rhythm—
their ornate vestments all candescent—
my thoughts turn to all that's grand, that honors our race,
to our glory, our civilization—Byzantium.

Very Seldom

He's an old man. Spent, hunched over,
crippled by the years and lewd excesses,
he shambles slowly through the narrow street.
But once he's gone inside his house to hide
his wretchedness and his old age, he contemplates
what measure still belongs to him of youth.

Young men recite his lines now.
In their eyes, all alive, his visions rise.
Their healthy, sensual minds
and hard-lined, corded flesh
are moved by his revealing of the beautiful.

For the Shop

He wrapped them up carefully, neatly,
in precious green silk.

Roses of rubies, lilies of pearls,
violets of amethysts. Beautiful as he deems,

as he wished, as he sees they should be; not as he
saw them in nature or studies them. He'll leave them

in the cash-desk, signs of his bold and skillful work.
When some customer steps into the shop,

he brings out other things to sell—first-class ornaments—
bracelets, chains, necklaces, and rings.

Painted

I am careful in my work and love it.
But today composing—the slowness of it—has discouraged me.
The day has had a bad effect on me. Its shape
keeps growing darker. It's all wind and rain.
I'd rather see than say things.
I look in this painting, now,
at a beautiful boy who has lain down near a spring,
just where running must finally have tired him.
What a beautiful child: what a godly noon
to overtake him utterly and make him sleep.—
I sit and look in this way for a long time.
Immersed in craft again, I rest from all its labors.

Morning Sea

Let me stop here. Let me too look at nature, briefly.
The morning sea and cloudless sky
both deep shining blue, yellow shore; all
beautiful, immensely light.

Let me stop here. And let me, self-beguiling, seem to see them
(I saw them truly in the minute I first stopped);
and not here too my fantasies,
my memories, the idols of sensual joy.

Ionian

That we've smashed their statues,
that we've ousted them from their temples,
the gods have not died from any of this.
O land of Ionia, it's you they love still,
it's you their souls remember still.
When an August morning dawns over you,
your scented space gleams with their life;
and sometimes a young man's ethereal form,
vanishing, passing quickly,
crosses the tops of your hills.

At the Entrance to the Café

Something they said next to me
turned my attention to the entrance of the café.
And I saw the beautiful body that seemed like
Eros had made it at the crest of his skill—
molding the shapely limbs with joy;
marking a height for the sculpted frame;
moved when he created the face
and leaving, from the touch of his hands,
a feeling on the forehead, on the eyes and lips.

One Night

The room was poor and shabby,
hidden above the shady tavern.
From the window the view was an alley,
dirty and narrow. From below
came the voices of some workers
playing cards, having a good time.

And there on the common, the humble bed
I had passion's body, intoxicating joy
from sensual, rose lips—
rose lips of such an ecstasy
that writing now, after so many years,
in my solitary house, I'm drunk that way again.

Return

Return often and take me,
loved feeling return and take me—
when the body's memory awakes,
and old yearning goes through the blood again;
when the lips and skin remember,
and the hands sense that they touch again.

Return often and take me in the night,
when the lips and skin remember...

Far Off

I would like to speak of this memory...
But it's dimmed so now...it seems nothing's left of it—
because it lies far off, in my first years as a young man.

Skin as if made from jasmine...
On that August—was it an August?—night...
I almost remember the eyes now: they were, I think, deep blue...
Ah yes, that's right, deep blue: a sapphire blue.

He Swears

He swears every now and then to start a better life.
But when night comes with its own counsel,
with its own resolutions and its own promises—
but when night comes with its own power
of the body that wants and requires, he goes
back to the same fatal pleasure, lost, once again.

I Went

I shut myself away from nothing. Everything allowed, I went.
I went, through shining night,
to joyful gain,
half-actual, half-fashioned in the mind.
And I took strong wines to drink,
the same as the heroes of pleasure take.

Chandelier

In an empty and small room, just four walls
draped in all green cloths,
burns a beautiful, heat-haloed chandelier;
from that one light the flames each fire
a lewd ill, a salacious force.

In the small room that gleams candescent
from the chandelier's dazzling heat,
the light that's cast in no way is familiar.
The heat of this pleasure is not lit
for timid bodies.

POEMS: 1916–1918

Since Nine O'Clock—

Half past twelve. The time has passed quickly
since nine when I lit the lamp,
and sat down here. I've sat without reading
and without speaking. With whom could I speak,
all alone in this house?

The specter of my young body,
from when I lit the lamp at nine,
has come and found me and reminded me
of closed-up, aromatic chambers,
and past sensual delight—what brazen pleasure!
And it has also placed directly in my sight
streets which have now become unrecognizable,
lively, crowded nightclubs which have closed,
and theaters and cafés that existed, once.

The specter of my young body
came and also brought to me the source of sorrows;
the grief of familial life, separations,
feelings for those I come from and belong to,
feelings for the dead esteemed so slightly.

Half past twelve. How the time has passed.
Half past twelve. How the years have passed.

Understanding

My younger days, my sensual life—
how clearly I see their meaning now.

What needless regrets, what vanities...

But I didn't see the meaning then.

In the loose life of my early years
the aims of my poetry were taking shape,
the boundaries of my art were being drawn.

And that's why the regrets were never steady.
And my decisions to refrain, to change
lasted two weeks at the most.

Before the Statue of Endymion

On a white chariot which four mules
of purest white, adorned in silver, draw,
from Miletos I've come to Latmos. To perform
the sacred rites—sacrifices and libations—of Endymion
I've sailed from Alexandria in a purple trireme.—
And here is the statue. Now in ecstasy I behold
the famed beauty of Endymion.
My slaves empty baskets of jasmine; and auspicious
shouts of praise revive the pleasure of ancient days.

Envoys from Alexandria

They had not seen, for centuries, such fine gifts at Delphi
as these which had been sent from the two brothers,
the rival Ptolemaic kings. But, having received them,
the priests are nervous about the oracle. They'll need
all their experience to know how to word it precisely—
which of the two, which of such a pair should be offended.
And they convene at night in secret
and discuss the family affairs of the Lagids.

But see, the envoys are back. They're saying goodbye.
They say they're returning to Alexandria. And they don't
mention the oracle. The priests listen happily
(it's understood they will keep the splendid gifts),
but they're baffled, utterly,
not knowing what this sudden indifference means.
They're unaware that yesterday the envoys heard somber news.
The oracle had been declared at Rome; the thrones were allotted
    there.

Aristovoulos

The palace weeps, the king weeps,
inconsolably Herod the king mourns,
the whole town weeps for Aristovoulos,
who drowned—how senseless—accidently,
playing in the water with his friends.

And when they learn of it in other places,
when word goes up to Syria,
many of the Greeks will also be made sad:
as many as are poets and sculptors will mourn,
for Aristovoulos had been heard of among them,
and which of their aesthetically envisioned boys
ever came near the beauty of this child?
What statue of a god did Antioch ever merit
that matched this son of Israel?

She keens and weeps, the First Princess;
his mother, preeminent among the Hebrew women.
She keens and weeps, Alexandra, at the disaster.—
But when she finds herself alone, her sorrow changes.
She moans; she rages; she reviles; she curses.
How they've fooled her! How they've cheated her!
How their game is won at last!
They've wrecked the house of the Asmonaeans.
How did he manage it, that villain who is king;
that scheming, depraved, worthless man.
How did he manage it. What an infernal plot,
that even Miriam should have sensed none of it.
If Miriam had caught on, if she'd had suspicions,
she'd have found a way to save her brother;
she's a queen after all, she would have managed something.
How they'll vaunt now and gloat in secret,
the vicious ones, Kypros and Salome;

those debased women, Kypros and Salome.—
And that she's powerless, and compelled
to pretend she believes their lies:
that she's unable to go to the people,
to come out and shout to the Hebrews,
to say, to say how the murder happened.

Kaisarion

In part to get one epoch's details right,
in part to pass the time as well,
last night I picked up a book
of inscriptions honoring the Ptolemies.
The lavish praise and flattery
is similar for all of them. All are brilliant,
glorious, mighty, doers of good deeds;
everything they undertake surpassing wise.
When one mentions the women of the line, they too,
all the Berenices and the Cleopatras, are marvelous.

After I'd gotten the epoch accurately in mind
I'd have put the book aside if one brief reference
to the king Kaisarion, insignificant really,
hadn't suddenly caught my attention......

Ah, so you've shown up, with that vague
charm of yours. There are only a few lines
about you to be found in history,
and so my thought shaped you more freely.
I made you handsome and emotional.
My art gives your face
a dreaming, amiable beauty.
And I imagined every part of you, in such detail,
that late last night, as my lamp
went out—I let it go out deliberately—
I thought you came into my room,
it seemed to me you stood before me; as you
would have been in conquered Alexandria,
pale and weary, ideal in your sorrow,
still hoping compassion for you might stir in them,
the vile ones—who murmured, "Too many Caesars."

Nero's Term

Nero did not worry when he heard
what the Delphic oracle revealed.
"Seventy-three is an age he should fear."
He still had time to be happy.
He's thirty years old. The god
has given him a very ample term
in which to prepare for future dangers.

Now he'll go back to Rome a little tired,
but tired gloriously from that trip,
on which all the days were pleasure—
at theaters, in gardens, in gymnasiums...
Evenings in Achaia's cities...
Ah the pleasure of naked bodies above all...

That is Nero's portion. And in Spain Galba
secretly musters and drills his army,
the old man who's reached his seventy-third year.

In the Port

Young, twenty-eight, in a Tinean ship,
Emis made it to this port that serves inland Syria,
with a plan to learn the incense trade.
But he got sick on the voyage. And as soon
as he was put ashore, he died. His burial,
the poorest possible, took place here. A few hours
before he died he whispered something about "home,"
about "very old parents." But who they were no one knew,
nor what his homeland was in the Panhellenic world.
It's better so. Since this way,
although he lies dead in this inland port,
his parents will always hope that he's alive.

One of Their Gods

When one of them passed through Selefkia's market,
at the hour when darkness first comes on,
as would a tall and consummately handsome youth,
with the joy of invulnerability in his eyes,
with his black, perfumed hair,
those walking there looked, interested, at him,
and one would ask the other if he knew him,
and if he was a Greek from Syria, or a stranger.
But some, who observed with greater care,
understood and moved out of his way:
and as he vanished under the arcades,
in the shadows, in the evening's lights,
headed for the quarter that only lives
at night, with orgies and debauchery,
with every type of frenzy and abandon,
they speculated about which of Them he was,
and for which of his suspicious entertainments
he'd descended to the streets of Selefkia
from his Worshiped, his Most Venerated Halls.

The Tomb of Lanis

The Lanis that you loved is not here, Markos,
in this tomb where you come to cry, and where you stay for hours
    and hours.
The Lanis that you loved is nearer your side
when you withdraw to your house and see his portrait,
in which somehow is preserved whatever made him worthy,
in which somehow is preserved whatever you had loved.

Remember, Markos, the time you brought from the Proconsul's
palace the famous Kyrenean painter,
and how, as soon as he saw your friend, he wanted
to persuade you both, and with what an artist's cunning,
that he should do him, without question, as Hyacinth
(in that way word of his portrait would spread farther).

But your Lanis did not hire his beauty out like that;
and ironly opposed told him to present
neither Hyacinth, nor anyone else,
but Lanis, son of Rametichos, an Alexandrian.

The Tomb of Iasis

Here I lie, Iasis. The young man
famed, in this great city, for beauty.
The profoundly wise marveled at me; the superficial,
simple folk as well. And I rejoiced equally in both.

But the world regarded me so much as a Narcissus and a Hermes
that the excess depleted, killed me. Passerby,
if you are an Alexandrian, you will not condemn me. You know
the headlong rush our life is; what heat it has; what supreme pleasure.

In a Town of Osroini

From a tavern fight, where he was wounded,
they brought us our friend Remon, at about midnight yesterday.
From the windows, which we kept open wide,
the moon lit his beautiful body on the bed.
We're a mixture here: Syrians, Greeks, Armenians, Medes.
Remon's just the same. But yesterday,
when the moon lit his erotic face,
we all thought of the Platonic Charmides.

The Tomb of Ignatios

Here I am not the Kleon famous in Alexandria
(where they're not easily impressed)
for my houses, for my gardens,
for my horses and my coaches,
for the jewelry and the silks I wore.
All that's gone; I'm not that Kleon here;
let his twenty-eight years be extinguished.
I am Ignatios, chanter of the epistle, who recovered very late;
but even so, in that way I lived ten happy months
in the serenity and in the security of Christ.

In the Month of Athyr

With difficulty I read what's on this ancient stone.
"Lo[rd] Jesus Christ." I make out a "so[u]l."
"In the mon[th] of Athyr" "Leukio[s] fell a[sl]eep."
Where the age is cited, "He li[ve]d to the age of."
The Kappa Zeta indicates that he fell asleep young.
In the eroded spots I see "Hi[m] . . . Alexandrian."
Three lines follow very mutilated:
though I can pick out some words—like "our te[a]rs," "pain,"
afterward again "tears" and "to [u]s his [f]riends grief."
I gather that Leukios must have been greatly loved.
In the month of Athyr Leukios fell asleep.

For Ammonis, Who Died at 29, in 610

Raphael, they've asked you to compose
a few verses for the poet Ammonis's epitaph.
Something very decorous and refined. You will be able,
you are the one best suited to write as is fitting
for the poet Ammonis, one of us.

Obviously you will speak of his poems—
but speak as well of his beauty,
of his delicate beauty which we loved.

Your Greek is admirable and musical always.
But we desire all your skill perfected now.
Our sorrow and our love are passing into foreign speech.
Pour out your Egyptian feeling in the foreign speech.

Raphael, your verses must be so written
as to bear some of our life, you know, within them,
so that both the rhythm and each phrase declare
an Alexandrian is writing for an Alexandrian.

Aimilianos Monai, Alexandrian, 628–655 A.D.

With words, with appearance, and with manners
I'll make an excellent suit of armor;
and so I'll face malicious people
and have no fear or weakness.

They'll want to do me harm. But no one
will know, of all those who gather round me,
where my gashes lie, the spots I can be hurt in,
under the deceptions that will cover me.—

Words for deeds from a boasting Aimilianos Monai.
Did he ever really make that suit of armor?
In any case, he didn't wear it long.
At the age of twenty-seven, in Sicily, he died.

When They Surge, Excited

Try to keep them, poet,
though scarcely any can be made to stay.
The visions of your erotic life.
Put them, half-hidden, in your lines.
Try to hold them, poet,
when they surge, excited in your mind
at night or in the shining light of noon.

Pleasure in the Flesh

Joy and balm of my life, the memory of those hours
where I found and where I held pleasure as I wanted it.
Joy and balm of my life, that I turned displeased away from
every amusement of routine erotic touch.

I've Gazed So Long, So Much—

I've gazed so long, so much on beauty
that my vision is replete with it.

Lines of the body. Red lips. Voluptuous limbs.
Hair that seems taken from Greek statues;
always beautiful, though it be uncombed,
and falling, lightly, on white brows.
Faces and persons of love, as my poetry
needed them to be....in the nights of my youth,
in those nights of mine, furtive, secretly encountered......

In the Street

His amiable face a little pale;
his brown eyes gone all languid;
twenty-five years old, easily thought twenty;
with some artistic sense for dressing—
a color in the tie, the collar's shape—
purposeless, he walks along the street,
still hypnotized, it seems, by the lawless passion,
the very lawless passion which he has attained.

The Tobacco Shop Window

Near a bright-lit tobacco shop window
they stood, among many others.
Their glances met, randomly,
and fearing, hesitant, expressed
their flesh's outlawed desire.
A few anxious, sidewalk steps followed,
until they smiled, and nodded slightly.

And then came the closed coach....
the senses drawing in two bodies;
the hands united, and the lips.

Passing Through

Those things he pictured timidly while a schoolboy
are open, revealed there before him. And he circulates,
stays up all night, is taken in. And as is proper
(for our art) his blood, fresh and hot,
is pleasure's prize. Lawless, euphoric sex
conquers his body; and the youthful limbs
give way to it, resistless.

                                   And so, a mere boy
becomes one worth our seeing, and through
the exalted World of Poetry, for a moment, he too passes—
sensation's child, the one whose blood is fresh and hot.

In the Evening

Things would not have gone on long in any case.
Years of experience show that much to me.
Still, Fate came somewhat rushed to stop it.
That handsome life was brief.
But the fragrances, how strong they were,
how exceptional the bed we lay in,
to what passion, what delight we gave our bodies.

An echo from the days of pleasure,
an echo of the days came close to me,
something of our shared youth's fire:
Once more I took a letter in my hands,
and read again and then again until the light was gone.

And sad, I stepped out on the balcony—
stepped out to change my thoughts by seeing
at least a little of this beloved city,
a little life in the streets and in the shops.

Gray

Looking at a half-gray opal
I remembered two beautiful gray eyes
I'd seen; that must be twenty years ago . . . .

. . . .

For one month we were lovers.
Then he left, I think for Smyrna,
to take a job there, and we never saw one another again.

They'll have turned ugly—if he's living—the gray eyes;
the beautiful face will have become a ruin.

Keep them, you, my memory, as they were.
And, memory, whatever of that fleshly love
you can, whatever you can, bring back to me tonight.

Before the House

Yesterday, walking in a remote quarter,
I passed outside the house
I used to enter when I was very young.
Eros, with his magnificent force,
had seized my body there.

           And yesterday,
while I passed by on the old road,
immediately, by love's secret grace,
the shops, the sidewalks, the stones,
and walls, and balconies, and windows
all turned beautiful;
nothing there stayed ugly.

And while I stood and stared at the door,
while I stood and let time go slowly by the house,
the essential life in me let
all its guarded passion shine.

The Next Table

He can't be more than twenty-two years old.
And yet I'm sure that almost as many years
earlier I held this same body, in joy.

It's not in any way a flash of longing.
And I've only recently come into the casino;
I've had too little time to drink a lot.
I held this same body, in joy.

And if I don't remember where—my small forgetting doesn't matter.

Ah now, now that he's sat down there at the table next to mine,
I recognize all the ways he moves—and beneath his clothes
I see the limbs again, loved, naked.

Remember, Body...

Body, remember not only how much you were loved,
not only the beds where you lay down,
but also those desires that for you
shone openly in eyes,
trembled in a voice—and were thwarted
by some random hindrance.
Now that all of them are gone, closed inside the past,
it nearly feels as if you also gave yourself
to those desires—how they shone,
remember, in the eyes that looked at you;
how they trembled in the voice, for you, remember, body.

Days of 1903

I didn't find them again, ever—those lost so fast....
the poetic eyes, that pale face....
on the nighttime street....

I didn't find them after that—those gained
utterly by chance, which I so easily let go;
and afterward with anguish longed for.
Those poetic eyes, that pale face,
those lips I never found again.

POEMS: 1897–1908

excluded from

POEMS: 1905–1915

and POEMS: 1916–1918

Voices

Ideal and loved voices
of those who have died, or of those who are
as lost for us as the dead.

At times in our dreams they speak;
at times in thought the mind hears them.

And with their sound for a moment return
sounds from the first poetry of our life—
as music, at night, distant, that vanishes.

Desires

Beautiful bodies of the dead who did not age
and were closed up, with tears, in a mausoleum's opulence,
with roses at the head, and jasmine at the feet—
that is what desires resemble, those gone
without fulfillment, not one given
its erotic night, or one its shining morning.

Candles

Future days stand before us
like a row of small lit candles—
golden, warm, and vivid candles.

Days that have passed remain behind,
a pitiful line of spent candles;
the nearest are still smoking,
cold candles, melted, and bent.

I do not want to see them; and then sadly
remember the shape and light they started with.
I look directly to my lit candles.

I do not want to turn, lest I shudder when I see
how quickly that dark line lengthens,
how quickly the dead candles crowd together.

An Old Man

At the noisy heart of the café
an old man sits hunched at the table;
with a newspaper before him, with no companions.

And in the vile indignity of old age
he thinks how little he enjoyed the years
when strength and mind and beauty were all his.

He knows he's gotten very old; it fills his mind, he watches it.
The time when he was young, though, seems to him
like yesterday. How small the interval, how small the interval.

And he reflects on Temperance, on how it fooled him;
and how he always believed—what madness!—
that lying voice which said, "Tomorrow. You have lots of time."

He remembers passions that he checked; and how much
joy he sacrificed. His brainless wisdom,
each ruined chance derides it now.

... But from thinking and remembering so much
the old man fades, bewildered. And he nods off,
in the café, bent over at the table.

Prayer

To her depths the sea has taken a sailor.—
His mother, not knowing, goes and lights
a tall candle in front of the All Holy Mother,
for him to return quickly, and for good weather—
and her ear she keeps turned all to the wind.
But while she faithfully wishes and prays,
the icon listens, solemn and sorrowful,
knowing he won't ever come now, the son for whom she waits.

The Old Men's Souls

In their aged, ruined bodies
sit the souls of men grown old.
How sadly afflicted the poor things are,
and how heavy bored they are, enduring their life of misery.
How they tremble fearing to lose it, and how they love it,
the confused and contradictory
souls, who sit—tragicomical—
in their old, beleaguered husks.

The First Step

The young poet Evmenis
complained one day to Theocritus:
"Two years have now passed since I've been writing,
and I've done just one idyll.
It's my only finished piece.
Despairing, I see that Poetry's ladder
ascends high, very high;
and that from where I am here on the first rung,
I, unfortunate, never will ascend."
Theocritus said: "Those words
are impertinence and blasphemy.
You should be proud and happy
that you're even on the first step.
That you've gotten here is no small thing;
as much as you've done is a great glory.
Even this first step
leaves behind many of the world's common sort.
To step on this rung
you must in your own right belong
to the city of ideas.
And it's difficult and rare
to be sworn in by men there.
In her agora you find Legislators
that no charlatan ever fools.
That you've gotten here is no small thing;
as much as you've done is a great glory."

Interruption

What the gods enact we interrupt,
hasty and inexperienced, existing for the moment.
In the palaces of Eleusis and Phtia
Demeter and Thetis start good works
in high flames and deep smoke.
But Metaneira always rushes in
from the royal chambers, hair undone, terrified,
and Peleus always gets scared and intervenes.

Thermopylae

Honor to those who in their life
name and defend Thermopylae.
Never leaving what obliges them to stay;
just and direct in all of their actions,
but showing pity as well, and compassion;
generous whenever they are rich, and when
they are poor, generous again in small things,
once again contributing whatever they can manage;
at all times speaking the truth,
but without hatred for those who have made themselves liars.

And greater honor is due to them
when they foresee (and many foresee)
that Ephialtis will show up at the end,
and that the Medes at last will come crashing in.

Che Fece .... Il Gran Rifiuto

To certain people there comes a day
when they should say the great Yes
or the great No. An instant shows who holds
the Yes ready in himself, and saying it

he crosses into limitless honor and confidence.
The naysayer does not repent. If asked again,
he would repeat the no. But he's brought down
by that no—the fitting one—for all his life.

The Windows

In these dark rooms, where I go
through weary days, I wander back and forth,
looking for the windows.—When it opens,
a window will be consolation.—
But the windows aren't there to be found, or I'm unable
to find them. And perhaps it's better for me not to find them.
Perhaps the light will be some novel tyranny.
Who knows what new things it will show.

Waiting for the Barbarians

—What are we doing gathered in the bazaar, and waiting?

    The barbarians are supposed to get here today.

—Why are things so dead inside the Senate?
How can the senators just sit there, making no laws?

    Because the barbarians will get here today.
    What laws should the Senate pass at this point?
    The barbarians, when they come, will be making all the laws.

—Why did our emperor rise so early in the morning,
and why is he sitting in the city's grandest gate
on the throne, ceremonial, wearing the crown?

    Because the barbarians will get here today.
    And the emperor expects to receive
    their commander. In fact, he has prepared
    a parchment as a gift. There he's written him
    many titles and great names.

—Why, today, have our two consuls and our praetors
appeared in their red, embroidered togas;
why did they wear bracelets of so many amethysts,
and rings with gleaming, polished emeralds;
why, today, should they take up those precious canes
with exquisite carving in silver and gold?

    Because the barbarians will get here today;
    and such things dazzle barbarians.

—And why don't our accomplished orators come out,
as they always do, to make their speeches, and have their say?

Because the barbarians will get here today;
and that kind get bored with bombastic speeches.

—Why has this trouble broken out just now,
and panic? (Faces have gone so solemn.)
Why are the streets, the squares emptying so fast,
and all the people brooding as they turn back home?

Because night has come and the barbarians have not.
And a few people have come back from the outskirts,
and said no more barbarians exist.

So now what will become of us, without barbarians.
Those men were one sort of resolution.

Unfaithfulness

Then, though there are many other things that we praise in Homer, this we will not applaud . . . . nor shall we approve of Aeschylus when his Thetis avers that Apollo, singing at her wedding, foretold the happy fortunes of her issue,

> "Their days prolonged, from pain and sickness free.
>   And rounding out the tale of heaven's blessings,
>   Raised the proud paean, making glad my heart.
>   And I believed that Phoebus' mouth divine,
>   Filled with the breath of prophecy, could not lie.
>   But he himself, the singer . . .
>   Is now the slayer of my son."
>   —Plato, *Republic*

When Thetis and Peleus were married
Apollo arose at the splendid wedding
feast, and blessed the new bride and groom
for the son who would issue from their union.
He said: Illness never will touch him
and his life will be long.— When he said this,
Thetis rejoiced greatly, since the words of Apollo,
who knew what prophecy was,
seemed to her a pledge to safeguard her child.
And when Achilles grew up, when
all Thessaly took pride in his beauty,
Thetis remembered the god's words.
But one day old men came with news,
and told how Achilles was killed at Troy.
And Thetis tore her purple robes apart,
and took off and flung from herself
into the dirt her bracelets and rings.
And in her lament she remembered the past;
and she asked what wise Apollo was doing,

where was the poet sauntering who speaks
so sublimely at feasts, where was the prophet ambling
when they killed her son at the crest of his youth.
And the old men answered that this same Apollo
himself had come down to Troy,
and with the Trojans had killed Achilles.

The Horses of Achilles

Seeing that Patroklos was slaughtered,
who was so manly, strong, and young,
the horses of Achilles began weeping;
their deathless nature leapt in rage
at this accomplishment of death.
They waved their heads, and shook their long manes,
with their hooves they struck the earth, and lamented
knowing Patroklos was lifeless—ruined—
base flesh now—his mind lost—
undefended—breathless—
returning to the great Nothing out of life.

Zeus saw the deathless horses' tears
and pity moved him. "It was wrong,"
he said, "for me to act so carelessly at Peleus' wedding feast;
Not giving you would have been better, my poor horses!
What business did you have down there
with miserable mankind, the plaything of fate.
Exempt from death, exempt from age,
time's offending rule still subjects you.
Men have implicated you in their suffering."
And yet not that, but death's eternal ruin
still forced the tears from these two noble beasts.

Walls

Without regard, without pity, without shame,
massive and high all around me they've built walls.

And I sit here now and give up all hope.
I have no other thought: this fate gnaws at my mind;

because I had so many things to do out there.
Ah, when they constructed the walls, how could I have paid no
    attention.

But I never once heard a noise or any sound come from the builders.
Imperceptibly they've shut me away from the world out there.

The Funeral of Sarpedon

Zeus grieves mightily. Patroklos
has killed Sarpedon; and now
Patroklos, Menoitos's son, and the Achaians rush
to carry off the body and degrade it.

But Zeus does not consent at all to that.
His beloved child—whom he abandoned
to loss; such was the Law—
at the least he will honor him dead.
And behold, to the plain he sends down Phoibos,
instructed in how the body is to be cared for.

The dead hero, with reverence and pity,
Phoibos raises, and he takes him to the river.
He cleanses him of dust and blood;
he closes the horrible wounds, leaving
not a trace apparent; perfumes of ambrosia
he pours out over him; and with shining
Olympian garments dresses him.
The skin he colors white; and with a pearl
comb he combs the jet-black hair.
The beautiful limbs he straightens and lays down.

Now he looks like a young charioteer king—
in his twenty-fifth, in his twenty-sixth year—
at rest after he has won,
with an all-gold chariot and the fastest horses,
in a celebrated race, the prize.

When he had completed his command this way
Phoibos summoned the two brothers
Sleep and Death, ordering them
to take the body to Lykia, that rich country.

And for that rich country, Lykia,
these two brothers set off on foot,
Sleep and Death, and when at last they
reached the door of the regal house
they gave over the glorified body,
and went back to their other cares and work.

And when they had received him, in the house,
the grievous burial began; with processions and honors
and lamentations, with plentiful libations from sacred vessels,
and with everything decorum called for,
and later skilled workers from the city
and famed artisans in stone
came and made the tomb and pillar.

UNPUBLISHED POEMS: 1919–1932

The Afternoon Sun

This room, how well I know it.
Now this one and the one next door are leased out
as commercial offices. The entire house
has become offices for realtors, for salesmen and firms.

Ah this room, how familiar it is.

Here, close to the door, was the couch,
and in front of it a Turkish rug;
nearby the shelf with two yellow vases.
To the right; no, opposite, a wardrobe with a mirror.
A table in the center where he wrote;
and the three big wicker chairs.
Next to the window was the bed
where we loved so many times.

Somewhere the poor things still exist.

Next to the window was the bed;
in the afternoon the sun reached half across it.

...In the afternoon at four o'clock
we parted for just one week...Ah then sorrow,
that week became eternal.

To Abide

It was sometime near one at night,
or one-thirty.

        In a corner of the wineshop;
behind the wooden screen.
Except for the two of us the shop completely empty.
An oil lamp cast its small light.
In the doorway the wine clerk kept his watch asleep.

No one could have seen us. We, though,
were aroused so much already,
that we were senseless of precautions.

Our clothes opening up halfway—they were sparse,
since July was a month of exquisite heat.

Gratified flesh amidst
half-opened clothes;
flesh uncovered swiftly—whose ideal form
has crossed twenty-six years; and now
comes to abide in this poetry.

Of the Jews (50 A.D.)

Painter and poet, runner and discus-thrower,
beautiful as Endymion, Ianthis Antoninus.
From a family dear to the Synagogue.

"My most honorable days are those
when I shun the aesthetic quest,
when I abandon beautiful and demanding Hellenism,
with its reigning fixation
on consummately made perishable white limbs.
Then I become he whom I would like always to remain;
son of the Jews, the holy Jews."

Very fervent, his declaration. "Always
to remain of the Jews, of the holy Jews—"

But he did not remain such a man at all.
The Hedonism and Art of Alexandria
took him for their own devoted son.

Imenos

"...And yet more should be loved
the pleasure that comes as a malady, damaging:
this pleasure seldom discovers the body whose sensuous forces it
    needs—
that through malady, damaging, bestows
an erotic intensity which health cannot know..."

Extract from a letter
written by the young Imenos (born patrician), notorious
in Syracuse as profligate
in the profligate times of Michael the Third.

From the Ship

It's like him, surely, this small
picture of him, done in pencil.

Quickly done, on the ship's deck;
one magical afternoon.
The Ionian sea around us everywhere.

It's like him. Still, I remember him more handsome.
He was, almost to the point of affliction, an aesthete,
and that lit his expression.
He seems still more handsome to me
now that my soul calls him back, out of Time.

Out of Time. All these things are very old—
the sketch, and the boat, and the afternoon.

Of Dimitrios Sotir (162–150 B.C.)

His hopes, each one of them, turned out wrong!

He had imagined he would perform highly honored deeds,
so that the humiliation which from the time of the battle
of Magnesia had borne down on his country would cease.
Syria would thus once more become a powerful state,
with her armies, with her navies,
with grand fortresses, with riches.

He suffered, growing bitter in Rome
when he sensed in the talk of his friends,
the young men of the great families,
in all the finesse and courtesy
which they showed him, the son
of King Selefkos Philopator—
when he sensed nonetheless that there always existed
some hidden slighting of the hellenizing dynasties;
that they were finished, could do nothing that mattered,
that they were extremely unsuited to rule over nations.
He'd gone his own way, alone, exasperated, and he'd sworn
that what they believed soon would not be true at all:
anyone could see that he had strong aspirations;
he would struggle, he would achieve things, he would raise it all again.

He had to find some way to make it to the East,
arrange some secret flight from Italy—
and all this strength which he had
in his soul, all this cresting passion
he would impart then to the common people.

Ah if only he might find himself in Syria!
He left the homeland so young
that he remembered the look of her dimly.

But in his thought he dwelled on her always
as something holy that you approach in worship,
as a visionary place of beauty, as a mystic scene
of cities and harbors that are Greek.—

And now?
        Now hopelessness and grieving.
The fellows in Rome were right.
It is not feasible that the dynasties
which arose in the Macedonian Conquest should endure.

But what of that: he'd striven mightily,
he'd fought as long as he could.
And in his dark, blasted longing
there's only one thing he still observes with pride;
that even in his failure,
it's the same unconquerable bravery he shows to the world.

The other things—those were dreams and labors in vain.
This Syria—it almost doesn't seem his country,
this place is the land of Herakleidis and of Valas.

If Actually Dead

"What seclusion has the sage gone to,
where has he vanished?
After his many miracles,
the fame of his teaching
which spread to many nations,
he hid himself suddenly and no one knew for certain
what became of him
(nor did anyone ever see his tomb).
Some started rumors that he died at Ephesus.
But Damis didn't write of that; Damis wrote
nothing at all about the death of Apollonius.
Others said that at Lindos he became invisible.
Or perhaps that story
of his being lifted up in Crete
at the ancient sanctuary of Diktynna
is true—But then we have his wondrous,
his supernatural appearance to a young student at Tyana.—
Maybe the time hasn't come for him to return
and appear to the world again;
or maybe, transfigured, he moves among us
unrecognized.—But he will reappear
as he was, teaching the ways of truth; and then of course
he will restore the worship of our gods,
and our elegant Hellenic rites."

So, in his meager dwelling—
after reading Philostratos's
"On Apollonius of Tyana"—
mused one of the few,
the very few pagans still left. Nonetheless—
insignificant, cowardly man that he was—

he played the Christian in public and went to church.
It was the time when Justin the Elder
reigned in strictest piety,
and Alexandria, most godfearing,
detested wretched idolaters.

Young Men of Sidon (400 A.D.)

The actor they'd brought in to entertain them
also recited a few choice epigrams.

The hall opened onto the garden;
and held a soft fragrance of flowers
that fused with the scents
of the five young, perfumed Sidonian men.

There were readings from Meleager, Krinagoras, and Rhianos.
But when the actor recited,
"Aeschylus, son of Euphorios, lies here—"
(stressing perhaps more than was needed
that "thriving strength" and that "Marathonian grove"),
a fervent young man, fanatic
about literature, burst forward and shouted;

"I don't like that quatrain at all.
Expressions of that sort seem somehow like failures of spirit.
Give—I say—all of your strength to your work,
all of your care, and think again of your work
when you suffer hardship, or when you first grow old.
These things I expect of you and require.
And that you do not banish altogether from your brain
the shining Form of Tragedy—
what *Agamemnon*s, what marvels in *Prometheus*,
what performances of *Orestes*, of *Kassandra*,
of *The Seven Against Thebes*—and set down as your only memory
that in the ranks of soldiers, in the herd,
you also fought against Datis and Artaphernis."

That They Might Appear—

One candle will do. Such light, so faint,
becomes them more, will charm them more
when they appear, the Ghosts of Love.

One candle will do. The room tonight
must not shine. Rapt, musing
on evocations, all in a small light—
rapt, musing, so I will turn visionary
that they might appear, the Ghosts of Love.

Dareios

The poet Phernazis is shaping
the crucial part of his epic.
How Dareios, son of Hystaspis,
took over the Persian kingdom. (It's from him
that our glorious king, Mithridates,
Dionysus and Evpator, takes his descent.) But here
philosophy is called for; he has to analyze
the feelings Dareios would have had:
perhaps disdain and frenzy; no—more likely
some pure understanding of the vanities in greatness.
The poet thinks about the matter deeply.

But his servant interrupts him, entering
in a great rush, and announcing very important news.
The war with the Romans has started.
Most of our army has crossed the borders.

The poet's left bewildered. What a calamity!
How may our glorious king
Mithridates, Dionysus and Evpator,
concern himself with Greek poems now?
In the middle of a war—imagine, Greek poems.

Phernazis grows anxious, vexed. Bad luck!
He's poised now to succeed with *Dareios*,
definitively, and to silence
his envious critics for good.
Such delaying, such delaying of his plans.

Delay by itself might not be so bad.
But it remains to be seen whether we're
safe in Amisos. The town is no fortress.
The Romans are horrifying enemies, most horrifying.

Can we, Cappadocians, succeed against them?
Could it ever happen?
Are we to match our numbers against the legions?
Great gods, protectors of Asia, help us.—

But through all of his shock and turmoil,
the poetic idea also insistently comes and goes—
what's most likely, of course, is disdain and frenzy;
Dareios would have felt disdain and frenzy.

Anna Komnina

In the prologue to her *Alexiad*
Anna Komnina laments her widowhood.

Her soul is all vertigo. "And
I flood my eyes," she tells us, "now
gutters for tears.... Alas the waves" of her life,
"alas the uprisings." Grief burns her
"to the bones and marrow, to the rending of the soul."

But the truth seems to be that she only felt
one mortal blow, this woman in love with power;
she had only one deep-cutting sorrow
(even if she doesn't confess it), this haughty female Greek,
that she didn't manage, for all her cunning,
to acquire the kingship; that instead a man
took it, virtually out of her hands—one impertinent John.

A Byzantine Gentleman, in Exile, Composing Verses

The frivolous can call me frivolous.
In serious matters I've always been
the most diligent of men. And I'd also insist
that no one knows better than I do
the Holy Fathers or the Scriptures, or the Canons of the Synods.
Each time he was in doubt,
each time he found Church study difficult,
Botanaitis came for help to me, first to me.
But exiled here (may she rot, that spiteful
Irini Doukana), and horribly bored,
it is by no means unfitting to amuse myself
writing six- and eight-line verses—
to amuse myself with mythic poems
on Hermes, and Apollo, and Dionysus,
or the heroes of Thessaly and the Peloponnese;
and to compose the most proper iambics,
such as—you'll permit me to say—the learned
of Constantinople do not know how to compose.
This perfectionism may well be what's brought about their censure.

Their Origin

The fulfillment of their lawless pleasure
is done. They've stood up from the mattress,
and dressed hurriedly without speaking.
They leave separately, furtively from the house; and as
they step somewhat anxiously along the street, it seems
they suspect that something at the surface in them betrays
what sort of bed they've just lain down in.

Yet how the artist's life has gained.
Tomorrow, the day after tomorrow, or years later
the lines of power will be written whose origin was here.

The Favor of Alexander Valas

Oh I'm not upset that a chariot wheel
broke, and that I lost some laughable race.
I'll spend the night drinking choice wines,
and lying among lovely roses. Antioch's mine.
I am its most fabulous young man.
I'm Valas's weakness, the one he adores.
Tomorrow, you'll see, they'll say the contest wasn't fair.
(But had I been tasteless, had I commanded it secretly—they'd have
given first place to me, the flatterers, despite my limping chariot.)

Melancholy of Jason Kleander;
Poet in Kommagini; 595 A.D.

The aging of my body and my features
is a wound from a savage knife.
There's no enduring it.
Quickly I resort to you, Poetic Art,
for whatever you might know of drugs;
some narcotics for pain, in Fantasy and in the Word.

It is a wound from a savage knife.—
Bring your drugs, Poetic Art,
which take away—for just a bit—awareness of the wound.

Dimaratos

His topic, the Character of Dimaratos,
which Porphyrios proposed to him in conversation,
was phrased this way by the young sophist
(who intended, later, to develop it rhetorically).

"A courtier, first of King Dareios,
and afterward of King Xerxes;
now with Xerxes and his army,
now at last Dimaratos will be vindicated.

"Great injustice had been done to him.
He was son to Ariston. Shamelessly
his enemies had bribed the oracle.
And just to take away his crown was not enough for them,
even when he'd finally removed himself,
and stoically resolved to live as a private citizen,
they felt the need at once to slander him before the people,
they felt the need to humble him in public at the festival.

"So he serves Xerxes with great zeal.
Along with the large Persian army,
he too will go back again to Sparta;
and king then, as before, how quickly
he will oust him, how low
he'll bring that scheming Leotychidis.

"And his days press on, full of anxiety;
he must advise the Persians, explain
what they should do to conquer Greece.

"Many arrangements, much thought, and this accounts
for Dimaratos's days being so tedious;
many arrangements, much thought, and this accounts

for Dimaratos having not a single moment's joy;
for what he feels isn't joy
(it is not; he can't say it's that;
how can he call it joy? his wretchedness has peaked)
when things show him clearly
that the Greeks will end up winning."

I've Brought to Art

I sit dreaming. I've brought
desires and the senses to Art—some things half-seen,
faces or lines; imperfect loves,
some vague memories. Let me entrust myself to Art.
Art knows how to bring together Beauty's forms;
almost imperceptibly making life full,
composing impressions, composing the days.

From the School of the Renowned Philosopher

He stayed a student of Ammonias Sakkas for two years;
but he grew bored both with philosophy and with Sakkas.

After that he entered politics.
But he abandoned that. The Eparch was an imbecile;
and those around him ceremoniously formal,
soberly comported dolts; louts, with triplicate barbaric Greek.

Something in the Church charmed
his curiosity; he would be baptized
and pass for Christian. But he quickly
changed his mind. He would surely have
soured things with his parents, ostentatious pagans,
and they would have immediately cut off—
a terrifying concern—their very liberal stipend to him.

But still, he needed to be doing something.
He became a regular in Alexandria's
corrupt houses, every hidden, debauched pit.

Here his luck came through for him;
it had given him a form of utmost beauty.
And he rejoiced in the godly gift.

At least for ten more years
his beauty would last. Afterwards—
perhaps he'd start from scratch again with Sakkas.
And if, in the meanwhile, the old man had died,
he'd go to some other philosopher or sophist;
someone suitable can always be found.

Or in the end he possibly
could still go back to politics—
commendably mindful once again of his familial tradition,
what is owed the country, and other noisy maxims.

Craftsman of Winebowls

On this winebowl of pure silver—
which was made for the house of Herakleidis,
where good taste governs perfectly—
behold: elegant flowers, and streams, sprigs of thyme,
see also in the midst how I have placed a handsome youth, naked,
erotic; he keeps one shin in the water still.—
I prayed, oh Memory, that I'd find you a perfect aid,
and so make the young man I loved the figure that he was.
Great hardship was involved, since fifteen years or so had passed,
from the day he fell, a soldier, in the defeat at Magnesia.

Those Who Fought for the Achaian Alliance

Brave you were who fought and died acclaimed;
those winning everywhere aroused no fear in you.
Blameless you, though blame was rightly placed on Diaios and
    Kritolaos.
When Greeks shall want to boast,
"This kind our nation breeds," they'll say
of you. Your praise will be such marveling.—

Written in Alexandria by an Achaian;
in the seventh year of Lathyros, a Ptolemy.

Before Antiochus Epiphanis

The young Antiochian said to the king,
"My heart pulses now with a cherished hope;
The Macedonians, Antiochus Epiphanis,
the Macedonians are back in the great fight.
Let them only win—and I'll give anyone who wants them
the lion and the horses, the Pan done all in coral,
and the elegant palace, and the gardens in Tyre,
and whatever else you've given me, Antiochus Epiphanis."

Perhaps in some small way the king was moved.
But he remembered instantly his father and his brother,
and made no response. An eavesdropper
could have picked up something.— And besides, naturally,
the terrifying end came fast at Pydna.

In an Old Book—

In an old book—close to a hundred years old—
forgotten between the pages,
I found a watercolor, without any signature.
It must have been the work of a surpassingly powerful artist.
It bore, as its title: "The Appearance of Eros."

But it was better interpreted: "—the eros of consummate sensualists."

Since it was apparent as you looked at the work
(the artist's conception was easily grasped)
that the young man in the drawing was not intended
for those who love somehow healthily,
who abide by what is manifestly permitted—
with chestnut, deep-shaded eyes;
with elite beauty in his face,
the beauty of an attraction far outside the norm;
with his ideal lips that bring
flesh's joy to the beloved body;
with his ideal limbs formed for beds
the current morality finds shameful.

Desperation

He's lost him utterly. And now he seeks
in the lips of every new lover
his lips; held by every new lover
he seeks to be deceived
that it's the same youth, that he gives himself to him.

He's lost him utterly, as though he never existed.
Since he wanted—that one said—wanted to be saved
from the sin-marked, deathly pleasure;
from the sin-marked, the disgraceful pleasure.
There was still time—as he said—for him to be saved.

He's lost him utterly, as though he never existed.
In fantasies, in hallucinations,
on the lips of other youths he searches for his lips;
he wanders seeking to feel his passion, his love again.

Julian, Seeing Contempt

"Having witnessed much contempt extant
among us toward the gods"—he says with a serious air.
Contempt. Well, what did he expect?
Let him organize religion as much as he liked,
let him write to the High Priest Galatios as much as he liked,
or to others of that ilk, urging and directing.
His friends weren't Christians;
definitely not. But even so, they couldn't
play as he could (brought up a Christian)
with a new ecclesiastical system,
laughable both in thought and in application.
They were Greeks after all. Nothing in excess, Augustus.

Epitaph of Antiochus, King of Kommagini

Having returned sorrowing from his funeral,
the sister of restrained and gentle
Antiochus, scholar and king of Kommagini,
wanted an epitaph for him.
And the Ephesian sophist Kallistratos—a frequent
resident in the small state of Kommagini,
gladly, hospitably, and often
received in the house of the King—
wrote it, advised by the Syrian courtiers,
and sent it to the now aged maiden.

"People of Kommagini, let the fame of beneficent
Antiochus the King be celebrated worthily.
He was a provident ruler of the country.
He lived a just man, wise, magnanimous.
He was also that best of things, Hellenic—
mankind has no quality more precious;
everything beyond that belongs to the gods."

Theater of Sidon (400 A.D.)

An honorable citizen's son—chiefly, a good-looking
young man of the theater, with versatile powers to please,
I sometimes compose, in Greek,
utterly scabrous verses, which I naturally
circulate very secretly—Gods! may they not see them,
those who go about darkly clothed mouthing morality—
verses of an exceptional pleasure, one that leads
to barren love and to opprobrium.

Julian in Nicomedia

Things far off the mark and full of high risk.
Commendations of the Greek ideals.
Theurgy, and visits to Pagan temples.
Enthusiasms for the ancient gods.
The constant speaking to Chrysanthios.
Theories of the philosopher—a clever one—Maximus.
And here's the result. Gallos is showing signs
of great uneasiness. Konstantios has certain suspicions.
Ah, the counselors were not in the least judicious.
This chronicle—says Mardonios—is overdone,
and the furor it's caused must be quelled, utterly.
Once more Julian returns, as liturgical reader,
to the church in Nicomedia,
where, full-voiced and ostentatiously reverent,
he intones the Holy Scripture,
and the laity marvel at his Christian piety.

Before Time Could Change Them

Great sorrow and regret overcame them on their separation.
It wasn't their desire; it was circumstances.
The need one had to earn his living
made him go far away—New York or Canada.
Their love, of course, was not the love they'd started with;
the attraction holding them by slow degrees had waned,
the attraction had waned to a great degree.
But that they should separate, that wasn't their desire.
It was circumstances.—Or perhaps Fortune
came on the scene as artist, separating them now,
before their feeling could vanish, before Time could change them;
the one will seem eternally what he was to the other—
a twenty-four year old; a young, a handsome man.

He Came to Read—

He came to read. There are
two or three books open; by historians and poets.
But he scarcely read ten minutes,
and abandoned them. He's dozing
on the couch. He is given entirely to books—
but he's twenty-three, and very handsome,
and this afternoon longing surged
through his ideal flesh, his lips.
Ardor surged, desire ran
through his flesh, beautiful everywhere;
with no absurd shame in the satisfaction's form.

31 B.C. in Alexandria

From his small village near the outskirts,
still dust-covered from the journey,
the peddler's arrived in town. And "Incense!" and "Gum!"
"The best olive oil!" "Perfumes for your hair!"
he calls out in the streets. But in the vast tumult
of music and parades what chance has he to be heard.
The crowd shoves him, it pulls him, it batters him.
And when he asks, now totally confused, "What is this insanity?"
someone tosses to him as well the huge lie
put out by the palace—that Antony's winning in Greece.

John Kantakuzinos Triumphs

He sees the fields that still belong to him,
the wheat, the animals, the fruit trees in them.
And farther off his ancestral home,
full of clothes, precious furniture, silverware.

They'll take them from him—Lord Jesus!—they'll take them from
   him now.

Might Kantakuzinos pity him
if he goes to fall at his feet. They say he's lenient,
very lenient. But those around him? And the army?—
Or, should he prostrate himself before Lady Irini, and moan there?

Fool! to get involved with Anna's faction—
if only Lord Andronikos had not lived long enough
to marry her. Have we seen
anything she's done end well, have we seen her once humane?
By now even the Franks no longer respect her.
Her plans were laughable, her entire strategy stupid.
While they were threatening everyone from Constantinople,
Kantakuzinos demolished them, Lord John demolished them.

And that he'd planned to join Lord John's
party! He would have done it too. And he'd have been happy now,
a great personage in all ways, firmly established,
if the bishop hadn't dissuaded him at the last moment,
with that hieratic, all-compelling stance of his,
his utterly fallible sources and news,
with his promises, and his idiocy.

Temethos, Antiochian; 400 A.D.

Lines of the young Temethos madly in love.
With the title, "Emonides"—Antiochus Epiphanis's
beloved companion; a surpassingly beautiful
young man from Samosata. But if the lines were made
fervent, rays of feeling, it's because Emonides
(from that other ancient epoch;
the 137th year of the Greek kingdom!—
maybe a bit earlier) appears in the poem
merely as a name; a suitable one, however.
The poem expresses a love in Temethos,
beautiful and worthy in him. We the initiated
friends close to him; we the initiated
know for whom the lines were written.
The unsuspecting Antiochians read the name, Emonides.

Of Colored Glass

I'm very moved by one detail
in the crowning, at Vlachernai, of John Kantakuzinos
and Irini, daughter of Andronikos Asan.
As they had no more than a few precious stones
(our afflicted empire was very poor),
they wore artificial ones. Numerous pieces made of glass,
red, green, or blue. There's nothing
humbling or undignified,
from my view, in those shards
of colored glass. They seem, on the contrary,
like a grief-struck protest
against the unjust fate of those crowned.
They are the symbols of what it was they should have had,
of what most certainly was proper for them to have
at their coronation—a Lord John Kantakuzinos,
a Lady Irini, daughter of Andronikos Asan.

The 25th Year of His Life

He goes regularly to the taverna
where they'd met the month before.
He asked; but they knew nothing.
From words they used, he understood that he'd met
one of those men nobody knows;
one of the many unfamiliar and untrustworthy
young faces passing through that place.
But he still goes regularly to the taverna, at night,
and sits there watching the doorway;
watching, till he's exhausted, the doorway.
Maybe he'll come through it. Tonight, perhaps, he'll come.

He does this for nearly three weeks.
His mind's sick now with lust.
On his mouth the kisses live still.
His flesh, all of it, is dying in that constant passion.
That man's body, its touch, covers him.
He wants to be joined with it again.

He tries (that's understood) not to give himself away.
But sometimes he almost doesn't care.—
Besides, he knows what he's risking,
he's accepted all that. It's not unlikely that this life of his
will lead him into devastating scandal.

On an Italian Shore

Kimos, son of Menedoros, a young Greek-Italian,
has made his life a sequence of good times;
as is the fashion for those young men from Greater Greece
brought up surrounded by vast wealth.

But today he is, despite his nature,
very thoughtful, sad. Near the shore,
deeply melancholic, he watches as they unload
ships with booty brought from the Peloponnese.

Greek spoils; booty from Corinth.

Ah today surely it isn't just,
it isn't possible for the young Greek-Italian
to give any longing thought to diversion.

In the Dull and Gloomy Village

In the dull and gloomy village where he works—
clerk in a shop selling clothes;
very young—and where he waits
for two, for three months more to pass,
two or three months more for business to go slack
and let him go off to the city to throw himself
into that scene, into those pleasures right away;
in the dull and gloomy village where he counts the hours—
he's gone to bed tonight in passion's grip,
all his youth lit bright by flesh's longing,
a beautiful new strength for all the beauty of his youth.
And in his sleep pleasure has come to him;
in sleep he sees and holds the form, the flesh he wanted....

Apollonios of Tyana in Rhodes

Apollonios was speaking
about suitable learning and upbringing
with a young man who was building a luxury house
in Rhodes. "When I enter a temple,"
the Tyanan said finally, "I greatly
prefer, even in a small one, seeing
a statue of ivory and gold
over seeing, in a large one, some figure of clay, all base."—

What's made "of clay" and "base;" disgusting:
still some (without adequate training)
are deluded by the hoax. What's made of clay and base.

The Illness of Kleitos

Kleitos, a likable young man,
about twenty-three years old—
with an excellent education, a rare knowledge of Greek—
is gravely ill. The fever's reached him
that cut a swath this year through Alexandria.

The fever found him already morally exhausted
from sorrow that his companion, a young actor,
had stopped loving and wanting him.

He's gravely ill, and terror's wracked his parents.

And an old servant who raised him,
she too fears for Kleitos's life.
Frantic for some remedy,
she brings to mind an idol
she worshiped as a girl, before she entered there, a servant,
in the house of distinguished Christians, where she too became a
    Christian.
Secretly she carries off some little cakes, and wine and honey.
She takes this before the idol. She chants pleas,
as many as she recalls; melodic bits and pieces. The fool
doesn't understand how little it matters to the black demon
whether or not a Christian recovers his health.

In a Township of Asia Minor

The news about the outcome of the sea-battle, at Actium,
certainly was unexpected.
But there's no need for us to draw up a new proclamation.
The name alone should be changed. Instead, there
in the final line, of "Having freed the Romans
from the disastrous Octavian,
that parody of a Caesar,"
we now will put "Having freed the Romans
from that disastrous Antony."
All the text fits handsomely.

"To the victor, the most highly glorified,
the, in every work of war, insuperable,
the marveled at for grand political achievements,
Antony, to whom, and for whose sake,
the township ardently wished victory"
here, as we said, the change: "Octavius,
whose victory the township holds as Zeus's finest gift—
to the puissant guardian of the Greeks,
whose favor makes Greek customs ever steadfast,
the dearly loved in every land that's Greek,
the one in whom distinction calls forth at once the highest praise,
and whose feats deserve extensive histories
in the Greek language, both metered and in prose:
in the Greek language, which is the vehicle of fame,"
et cetera, et cetera. It all fits brilliantly.

Priest at the Serapeion

My good father grown old,
he who loved me ever the same;
my good father grown old I mourn,
who died two days ago, shortly before dawn.

Jesus Christ, to keep the commandments
of your most holy church
in every deed of mine, in every word,
in every thought, is what I strive for
all the days of my life. And as many as deny you,
them I shun.—But now I mourn:
I grieve, O Christ, for my father,
for all that he was—a fearful thing to say—
at that thoroughly accursed Serapeion, a priest.

In the Wineshops—

I wallow in the wineshops and brothels
of Beirut. I did not want to go on living
in Alexandria. Tamides left me;
and went off with the Eparch's son to acquire
a villa on the Nile, a grand house in the city.
It was not fitting that I should go on living in Alexandria.
I wallow in the wineshops and brothels
of Beirut. I conduct my life dishonorably,
in base, corrupt abandon. The only thing redeeming me,
like enduring beauty, like perfume that has held on to my flesh,
is that for two years I had Tamides as my own,
the most splendid of all the young men,
as my own; not for a house or a villa on the Nile.

A Grand Procession of Priests and Laymen

Composed of priests and laymen, a procession,
all trades represented,
passes through streets, through squares and gates
of the renowned city, Antioch.
In this imposing, grand procession, in the front,
beautiful, white-clad, a boy holds
in upraised hands the Cross,
strength and hope for us, the Holy Cross.
The pagans, those recently so arrogant,
brought low now, cowards, draw
hastily apart from the procession.
Far from us, far from us may they always stay
(as long as they will not renounce their error). Forward
goes the Holy Cross. To every quarter
where Christians live in piety
it brings comfort and joy:
they come, the faithful, to the doors of their houses
and full of exultation do it reverence—
the strength, the salvation of the universe, the Cross.—

It is a yearly Christian holiday.
But today it is carried out, oh see, more openly.
The state at last has been redeemed.
The foul, the abominable
Julian reigns no longer.

For the most pious Jovian let us pray.

Sophist Departing from Syria

Estimable sophist, now that you are departing from Syria,
and planning to write about Antioch,
it's worth your mentioning Mebis in your work.
The renowned Mebis, who without question
is the best-looking young man, and the most beloved,
in all of Antioch. Not one of the other
boys in that life, none of them, is paid
as highly as he is. So they can have Mebis
only for two days, or three, men often give him
up to one hundred staters.—I've said, in Antioch;
but in Alexandria as well, and, surpassing even that, in Rome
one will not find a boy as enchanting as Mebis.

Julian and the Antiochians

Neither Chi, they say, nor Kappa ever harmed the city.... We
finding interpreters.... learned that these are the initial letters of
names, the first of Christos and the second of Konstantios.
    —Julian, *Misopogon* (Beard-Hater)

Was it ever possible they would renounce
their beautiful way of life; the variety
of their daily pleasures; their brilliant
theater, where one thing was made of Art
and their flesh's erotic bent!

Immoral to a degree—and probably to a great degree—
they were. But they had the satisfaction that their life
was the notorious life of Antioch,
pleasure-steeped, the connoisseur's ideal.

Were they to renounce these things, and be concerned with what
    then?

His airy mouthings about the false gods,
his boring, egocentric maxims;
his phobia, a child's, of the theater;
his graceless prudery; his ridiculous beard.

O certainly they cared more for Chi,
O certainly they cared more for Kappa—a hundred times more.

Anna Dalassini

In the royal decree that Alexios Komninos
issued especially to honor his mother,
the highly intelligent Lady Anna Dalassini—
she distinguished in her deeds and values—
there are diverse encomia:
from those let me offer here
one lovely, noble phrase:
"Not 'mine' nor 'thine,' neither cold word, did she ever say."

Days of 1896

He was fully debased. A sexual drift in him,
firmly prohibited and despised
(inborn for all that), was the cause:
society was very prudish.
Gradually he'd lost his little bit of money;
afterwards his place and his esteem in the community.
He would turn thirty soon, and not have spent a year
in any job, at least not in one that could be acknowledged.
Sometimes he covered his expenses
by brokering arrangements seen as shameful.
He finally became the sort of man who, if others
saw you with him often, could compromise you greatly.

But no, not just those facts; that would not be right.
The memory of his beauty deserves much more than that.
There is another view, and when he's seen in it,
he looks appealing; he seems the simple and genuine
child of eros, who above honor
and his reputation placed, unquestioning,
his pure flesh, pure sensual pleasure.

Above his reputation? But society,
which was very prudish, disposed things stupidly.

Two Young Men, 23 to 24 Years Old

From half past ten he'd been at the coffeehouse,
expecting him to appear soon.
Midnight had passed—and he was waiting for him still.
One-thirty had just passed; the coffeehouse
had emptied almost entirely.
He'd tired of reading the papers mechanically.
Of his desolate three shillings,
one alone remained: having waited so long,
he'd spent the others on coffees and brandy.
He'd smoked all of his cigarettes.
He was exhausted by all that waiting.
Since, alone as he was for hours, tiresome
thoughts had also started to take hold of him,
concerning the lapses in his moral life.

But when he saw his friend coming in—immediately
weariness, boredom, thought all left.

His friend brought unexpected news.
He'd won sixty pounds playing cards.

Their handsome faces, their cresting youth,
that love of the senses each felt for the other,
were refreshed, came alive, energized
by the sixty pounds from the card game.

And all joy and strength, sensation and beauty,
they went off—not to the homes of their honorable families
(where they were, after all, no longer wanted):
they went off to a very special bordello
well known to them, and asked for a bedroom
and expensive drinks, and drank again.

And when the expensive drinks were all finished,
when it was just about four in the morning,
they gave themselves, happy, to love.

Greek from Ancient Times

Antioch boasts of its splendid buildings,
and its lovely streets; of the marvelous
countryside around it, and of its vast,
teeming population. It boasts of being the seat
of glorious kings; and of the artists
and the sages it has, and of its immensely wealthy
and sensible tradesmen. But far beyond
all these, Antioch prides itself on being from ancient
times a Greek city; a relative of Argos:
through Ione, which was founded by Argive
colonists in honor of the daughter of Inachos.

Days of 1901

This is what was exceptional in him,
that in all his abandon
and all his rich sexual experience,
despite all the accustomed poise
that matched his bearing to his years,
there happened to be moments—
extremely rare, of course—when he gave the impression
his flesh had almost never been touched.

His twenty-nine-year-old beauty,
sampled so much for pleasure,
at moments strangely brought back the youth
who, somewhat ineptly, surrenders
his chaste body to love for the very first time.

You Didn't Understand

Of our religious beliefs,
the inane Julian said, "I read, I understood,
I condemned." As if he'd annihilated
us with his "condemned," the buffoon.

Wisecracks of that kind, however, have no impact
on us, the Christians. "You read, but you didn't understand; had you
understood, you wouldn't have condemned" was our immediate reply.

A Young Man, a Writer—in His 24th Year

Any way you can work now, brain.—
He's being injured by a half-lived joy.
He's in an exasperating position.
He kisses the beloved face each day,
his hands move over the most splendid limbs.
He has never loved with such immense passion.
But the beautiful fulfillment of eros is not there;
that fulfillment which needs two who long with one intensity.

(The two are not given equally to irregular sensual joy.
It ruled fully only in him.)

And he's dissipated, utterly unnerved.
Besides, he's also out of work; and that counts heavily.
With difficulty he borrows small amounts (sometimes he
comes close to begging for them), and makes a kind of living.
He kisses the worshiped lips; on the splendid body—
which he knows now merely allows him—he pleases sense.
And afterwards he drinks and smokes; drinks and smokes;
and drags along through cafés for whole days,
bored, he drags along the craving shot through all his beauty.
Any way you can work now, brain.

In Sparta

He didn't know, King Kleomenis, he didn't dare—
he didn't know how to say something like that
to his mother: that Ptolemy demanded
as fulfillment of their agreement that she be sent as well
to Egypt and be held as hostage there;
a very humiliating, unbefitting thing.
He'd always verge on speech; and always pause.
He'd always start to talk; and always he would stop.

But the excellent woman understood him
(by then she'd heard some rumors bearing on her fate),
and she encouraged him to be direct with her.
And she laughed; and said that certainly she'd go.
Indeed, she rejoiced that in
her old age she still could be of use to Sparta.

As for the humiliation—she simply set it by.
Certainly a Lagid, arriviste,
lacked all ability to comprehend the Spartan character;
and so his demand could not
in any real sense humiliate a Lady
of her eminence; the mother of a Spartan king.

Picture of a Young Man, Twenty-three,
Done by His Friend of the Same Age,
an Amateur

He finished the picture yesterday noon. Now
he looks at it in close detail. He showed
him in a gray, unbuttoned jacket, deep gray; without
a vest and tie. With a rose
shirt; open, so some part would shine out
of the beauty in his chest, his neck.
His hair on the right covers almost all
his forehead, his beautiful hair
(as the style he prefers this year requires).
Throughout there is the tone of sense's rapture
he wanted to impart when he did the eyes,
when he did the lips... His mouth, the lips
for yielding choice erotic joy.

In a Large Greek Colony, 200 B.C.

That things aren't what they should be in the Colony,
not the slightest doubt remains,
and even though we're moving forward somewhat,
perhaps, as not a few believe, the time has come
to bring in a Political Reformer.

The impediment, however, the difficulty
is that they make a huge issue
of everything, these Reformers.
(What a blessing it would be
if no one ever needed them.) To every item,
to the smallest fact they put tests and questions,
and they think up drastic remedies, at once,
with requirements attached for action with no delay.

They also favor sacrifices.
Give up that property of yours;
your possessing it is risky:
just such properties as these injure Colonies.
Give up that revenue,
and the other flowing from it,
and this third one: as a natural sequence;
they're clearly essential, but what else can be done?
they generate an adverse liability for you.

And the further they go with their investigation,
the more they find superfluous, the more they want an end to;
things, however, that one finds difficult to abolish.

And when, safe at last, they finish the work,
and, everything hemmed in, reduced to the last detail,
they go away, also taking away their just wages,
then let's see what's left, after
such surgical craft.—

Maybe the time hasn't come yet.
We should not rush; haste is a dangerous thing.
Premature measures bring regrets.
Disorder abounds, certainly and sadly, in the Colony.
But is there anything belonging to mankind without its flaw?
And, after all, look, we're making progress.

A Prince from Western Libya

He was generally liked in Alexandria
the ten days he stayed there,
the prince from Western Libya,
Aristomenis, son of Menalaos.
His attire, like his name, decent, Greek.
He accepted honors happily, but
he didn't require them; he was unassuming.
He bought Greek books,
in particular history and philosophy.
More than anything a man who spoke little.
His thoughts were likely deep, so the talk went,
and it was the nature of those types not to say much.

He was not given to depth in thought, or anything.
An accidental, trifling man.
He took a Greek name, dressed like the Greeks,
learned more or less to behave like the Greeks;
and his soul trembled that by chance
he'd spoil the tenuously good facade
with some barbaric, mangled speech in Greek,
and that the Alexandrians would revile him,
as is their habit, unforgiving.

And that is why he circumscribed his speech,
afraid and careful in grammar and pronunciation,
mad, almost, with the boredom of having
conversation heaped inside himself.

Kimon, Son of Learchos, Age 22,
Student of Greek Literature (in Kyrini)

"My end came while I was happy.
Ermotelis had me as his inseparable friend.
In my last days, for all his feigning
not to be upset, I still saw, often,
crying all around his eyes. Whenever he thought I'd
drifted off in sleep, he'd collapse, the way a man
distraught would, at the edge of my bed. We were, though, both
young men, the same age, twenty-three.
Fate is a traitor. Perhaps some different passion
might have taken Ermotelis from me.
I ended well; in an undivided love."

This epitaph for Marylos, son of Aristodemos,
dead one month ago in Alexandria,
I, mourning Kimon, cousin to him, received.
The man who wrote it sent it to me, a poet I know.
He sent it to me because he knew I was
a relative of Marylos: he knew nothing more.
My soul's replete with sorrow for Marylos.
We had grown up together, as brothers.
My heart aches. His premature death
extinguished completely every grudge . . . . .
every grudge I bore Marylos—for all
his having stolen Ermotelis's love from me,
so that even if Ermotelis might want me now once more,
it will not be at all the same. I know
my tender nature far too well. Idealized, Marylos
will come between us, and I'll feel him
say to me, "There you are, satisfied now.
There, you've taken him once more, as was your desire, Kimon.
There, you've no more cause to snipe at me."

On the March to Sinopi

Mithridates, glorious and powerful,
lord of great cities,
commander of mighty armies and fleets,
on his way to Sinopi made a long
detour to the rural
dwelling of a soothsayer.

Mithridates sent an officer of his
to ask the soothsayer how much more he would amass
in goods, what other powers, in the future, would be his.

He sent an officer of his, and after that
continued his march to Sinopi.

The soothsayer withdrew to a secret room.
After about half an hour he came out
ill at ease, and said to the officer;
"I am not satisfied, I could make nothing clear.
Today's not a propitious day.
I saw some shrouded things. I didn't grasp them well.—
But it's best, I believe, that the king find all he has sufficient.
Things added will be dangers to him.
Remember to tell him that, officer:
with all that he has, good God, let him be content!
Luck takes sudden turns.
Tell King Mithridates this:
one very rarely finds a man like his ancestor's noble
companion who, just in time, turns his spear's point
to the ground and writes salvation in the dust, *Flee Mithridates.*"

Days of 1909, '10, and '11

He was the son of a much wronged, penniless sailor
(from an island in the Aegean Sea).
He worked in the foundry. He wore ragged clothes.
His shoes were torn at work, pitiful.
His hands were filthy with rust and oils.

At evening, when the shop closed,
if there was something he wanted badly,
some tie just too expensive,
some tie for Sunday,
or if in a window he'd seen and pined
for some shop's blue shirt, lovely,
for five drachmas, or ten, he'd sell his body.

I ask myself whether in the ancient days
glorious Alexandria had any finer youth,
any perfection surpassing this boy—who was wasted:
no statue, of course, no picture was ever done of him;
thrown aside there in the iron-monger's squalid shop,
an unremitting job, and brutalizing, common men's
debauches quickly ruined him.

Myris: Alexandria, 340 A.D.

When I got word of the calamity, that Myris was dead,
I went to his house, much as I shun that,
entering the houses of Christians,
particularly when they grieve or celebrate.

I stood in a hallway. I did not want
to proceed in any further, since I observed
that the dead youth's relatives
looked at me with open suspicion and annoyance.

They had him in a large room
which, from the corner where I stood,
I saw a bit of: all precious carpets,
and vessels of silver and gold.

I stood and wept in a corner of the hallway.
And I thought that our meetings and excursions
would be worthless without Myris;
and I thought that I would never see him again
in our beautiful and salacious nights without sleep,
glad, laughing, and reciting verses
with his consummate sense of Greek rhythm;
and I thought of my loss forever
of his beauty, of my loss forever
of the young man whom I worshiped in abandon.

A few old women near me spoke quietly
about the last day he was alive—
on his lips, incessantly, the name of Christ,
his hands kept round a cross—.
Afterwards, four Christian priests
went into the room, and said prayers

zealously, and implored Jesus,
or Mary (I have no real knowledge of their faith).

We knew, of course, that Myris was a Christian.
Since the beginning, when he fell in with us
the year before last, we knew.
But he lived as we did, absolutely.
Of all our set the most given to gratification;
prodigally tossing out his money for diversions.
Indifferent to people's judgment,
he charged into any rumble that might break out
when our crowd ran up against
some different crowd at night.
He never spoke about his religion.
In fact, one time we told him
that we would take him with us to Serapeion.
But he seemed displeased
by our teasing; I remember now.
Oh, and two more occasions come back to me.
When we made libations to Poseidon,
he backed out of our circle, and turned his glance elsewhere.
When one of us, impassioned, said,
"Let our comradeship be in
the favor and protection of the great,
the supremely beautiful Apollo"—Myris whispered,
(the others did not hear) "With me as the exception."

The Christian priests with grand voices
prayed for the young man's soul—
I watched carefully with how much industry,
and with what close attention
to the rituals of their faith, they made everything
ready for the Christian funeral.
And suddenly an eerie feeling overcame me.

Vaguely, I sensed Myris near me, leaving;
I sensed that he was united, a Christian,
with his own kind, and that I was becoming
a stranger, I, very much a stranger; I also felt
a doubt encroaching: maybe I had been fooled
by my passion, and had always been a stranger to him.—
I burst out of their appalling house,
I went swiftly before it could be seized,
distorted by their christianity, the memory of Myris.

Alexandros Iannaios, and Alexandra

Successful and fully satisfied,
King Alexandros Iannaios,
and his spouse Queen Alexandra,
move forward proceeded by music
and panoplies of grandeur, luxury,
move forward through the streets of Jerusalem.
It's been accomplished brilliantly, the work
begun by the great Judas Maccabaios
and his four celebrated brothers;
work carried on without fail, through
many dangers, through many hardships.
Now nothing unbecoming has remained.
All obeisance to the arrogant
monarch of Antioch is over. Behold
King Alexandros Iannaios,
and his spouse Queen Alexandra,
in all ways equal to the Selefkids.
Good Jews, chaste Jews, first and foremost—loyal Jews.
But, also, as occasions demand,
adept at speaking Greek;
attuned both to Greeks and to hellenizing
monarchs—equal to them all though, that's to be known clearly.
Yes, it's been concluded brilliantly,
it's been concluded proudly,
the work begun by the great Judas Maccabaios
and his four celebrated brothers.

Flowers White and Beautiful,
as Were Most Becoming

He came into the café where they always went together.—
His friend had told him here, three months before,
"We haven't got five pence. We're two paupers,
you and I, forced into the low-cost clubs.
I'm being honest—I can't see you anymore.
Another man, accept it, wants me."
The other man had promised him two suits,
and several silk handkerchiefs. To get him back
the lover rampaged everywhere, and found twenty pounds.
The friend started things again with him for the twenty pounds:
but also, with the cash at hand, for their old companionship,
for their old love, for their depth of feeling.
The "other man" was a liar, a real bastard;
he'd provided one suit only, and he was forced
to that with ceaseless supplication.

Now, though, he has no more desire for suits,
and none at all for silken handkerchiefs,
and none for twenty pounds, and none for twenty piasters.

On Sunday they buried him, at ten in the morning.
On Sunday they buried him: it's been almost a week.

On his poor man's coffin he laid down flowers for him,
flowers white and beautiful, as were most becoming
to his beauty and to his twenty-two years.

That night when he went—some work came up,
something crucial to his livelihood—to the café
where they always went together; a knife in his heart,
that black café where they always went together.

Come, O King of the Lacedaimonians

Kratisikleia did not deign to let
the people see her weeping and lamenting;
and so she walked majestically, in silence.
Nothing showed in that calm face of hers
of the sorrow and the wrongs she suffered.
But even so, a moment came and she could not bear up;
before she stepped onto that wretched ship to go to Alexandria,
she took her son to the temple of Poseidon,
and when they were alone there she embraced
and kissed him. He was "lost in pain," says
Plutarch, "and remorseful."
Her strong character exerted itself though;
and, recovering, the marvelous woman
said to Kleomenis, "Come, O King
of the Lacedaimonians, as we go
out there again, let no one see us
weeping or doing anything at all unworthy
of Sparta. This belongs to us alone;
although the lots are given to infernal gods to cast."

And she stepped onto the ship, going toward that "given."

In the Same Space

The houses and cafés, the quarter,
surroundings that I've seen and walked through; year after year.

In joy, in sorrows I created you:
with so many episodes, with so many matters.

And you have made yourself entirely a feeling, for me.

The Mirror in the Vestibule

The opulent house had in its vestibule
a mirror, grand, and very old;
purchased eighty years ago at least.

A surpassingly beautiful boy, assistant to a tailor
(on Sundays an amateur athlete),
stood quietly by with a package. He handed it
to a servant of the house, and that man carried it inside
to bring back the receipt. The assistant to the tailor
was left alone, and waited.
He approached the mirror, looking into it,
and straightened his tie. Five minutes later
they brought him the receipt. He took it and he left.

But the old mirror that had seen and seen again,
in the many years of its existence,
thousands of things and faces;
the old mirror nonetheless exulted now,
and stood to its full proud height,
because it had displayed
beauty, in its entirety, for a few minutes.

He Asked about the Quality—

He left the office where he'd been taken on
at an unimpressive, low-wage rank
(his monthly pay around eight pounds: with perks),
came out when he had finished the lonely work
over which, all afternoon, he'd stooped:
came out at seven, and walked slowly,
idling in the road.—Handsome; and interesting:
having reached, as his demeanor showed,
absolute perfection in what sensation gives.
Just one month before, he'd turned twenty-nine.

He sauntered in the road, and in the poor
side streets that led to where he lived.

Passing in front of a small shop
where knock-off, low-priced goods
were sold to the working class,
inside he saw a face, he saw a form
that touched an urge in him, and he entered,
asking, as a cover, to see colored handkerchiefs.

He asked about the quality of the handkerchiefs
and what they cost; in a drowning voice,
extinguished, almost, by longing.
And the answers were returned in kind,
oblique, in a lowered voice,
with promised, closed consent.

The whole time they spoke randomly of the stock—
but to one end: to touch each other's hands
upon the handkerchiefs; to bring their faces

near, their lips, seemingly by chance;
to bring the limbs one instant's touch.

Hurriedly and furtive, so he wouldn't notice,
the place's owner, who was seated in its depths.

They Might Have Bothered

I've hit bottom, nearly homeless and penniless.
This fatal city, Antioch,
ate up all my money:
this fatal city, with its prodigal life.

Still, I'm a young man in perfect health.
I have astonishing command of Greek
(I know everything and more in Aristotle, in Plato;
in the orators, the poets, and in whatever you might cite).
I've some idea of military matters,
and connections in the senior mercenary corps.
I can handle administration.
Last year I spent six months in Alexandria;
I know enough (and this is useful) of the routine:
the maneuvering of Kagergetis, his swindling, and all the rest.

I believe therefore that I am abundantly qualified
to serve this country,
this dear fatherland of mine, Syria.

However they employ me, I'll strive to be
an asset to the country. That is my intention.
And if they balk me with their regular procedures—
we're on to them, these fine friends: why name them here?
if they balk me, I'm not to blame.

I'll approach Zabinas first,
and if that moron doesn't understand my value
I'll go to his rival, Grypos.
And if that idiot also doesn't take me on,
I'm off immediately to Hyrkanos.

In any case, one of the three will want me.

And my conscience is clear
in this indifferent choice.
They all damage Syria equally.

But how am I, a ruined man, to blame?
I'm down and out, just trying to patch a life together.
The almighty gods might have bothered
to create a fourth man who was good.
I would have happily attached myself to him.

Following the Formulas
of Ancient Greco-Syrian Magicians

"What potion's to be found, distilled from herbs
under a spell," said an aesthete,
"what distillation made following
the formulas of ancient Greco-Syrians
that for one day (if it can't stay
potent any longer) or for some small time
could bring my twenty-third year back to me
again; that could bring back to me again
my friend of twenty-two—the beauty and the love of him.

"What distillation's to be found, one made
following the formulas of ancient Greco-Syrian magicians,
that would, in keeping with the looking back,
restore as well our little room."

In the Year 200 B.C.

"Alexander, son of Philip, and the Greeks except the
    Lacedaimonians—"

We can very well imagine
how they'd have shown complete indifference
to this inscription in Sparta. "Except the Lacedaimonians,"
that's natural. The Spartans aren't the sort
to be led by others, to be commanded
like precious servants. Besides,
a pan-Hellenic expedition without
the reigning Spartan as commander
would not have seemed notable at all to them.
Yes, certainly, "except the Lacedaimonians."

That too is a position. Quite understandable.

So, except the Lacedaimonians at Granikos;
and after that at Issus; and in the decisive
battle that demolished the terrifying army
which the Persians mustered at Arbela:
which set out for victory from Arbela, and was demolished.

And from this marvelous pan-Hellenic expedition,
the triumphant, the effulgent,
the extolled, the glorified as
no other ever had been glorified,
the peerless: we emerged;
a new Greek world, magnificent.

We; the Alexandrians, the Antiochians,
the Selefkians, and the numberless
remaining Greeks of Egypt and of Syria,
and those in Media, and those in Persia, and all the rest.

With our widespread governance of many lands,
with a versatile process of judicious adjustment.
And the Common Greek Language
which we've carried as far as Bactria, as far as the Indians.

As if we'd mention Lacedaimonians now!

Days of 1908

That year he found himself without a job;
and consequently lived off cards,
off backgammon, and loans.

A position at three pounds monthly pay,
in a small stationer's, had been offered him.
But he refused it, without any hesitation.
It wouldn't do. That was no salary for him,
a young man decently educated, and twenty-five years old.

He won, or failed to win, from two to three shillings a day.
What could the fellow get from cards and backgammon
at the cafés of his set, the common man's,
however shrewdly he might play, however stupid the players he'd
    select?
The borrowing got worse and worse.
He came up, rarely, with a crown, mostly just a half,
and sometimes he'd settle for the lowest shilling.

For a week or so, at times longer,
when he could escape the late-night dread,
in the morning, at the baths, he'd refresh himself, then swim.

His clothes were terrifying ruins.
He wore one suit all the time,
a very faded cinnamon-toned suit.

Ah summer days of nineteen hundred eight,
in what you saw, expertly sensing beauty,
the faded cinnamon-toned suit was absent.

Your view has kept him what he was
when he took them off, when he cast them from him,
those unworthy clothes, that underwear in patches.
He stood then naked everywhere;
flawless in beauty; a miracle.
His uncombed hair upswept; his limbs touched sun-dark
from his morning naked at the baths and on the beach.

ONE EXTRA: 1933

In the Districts Surrounding Antioch

In Antioch we were perplexed on hearing
about Julian's latest behavior.

Apollo made things clear to him, at Daphni!
He'd no desire to hand out any oracle (we're worried!);
he'd no intention of speaking prophetically, unless
his temple in Daphni was cleansed first.
The neighboring dead, he declared, irritated him.

Abundant tombs may be found in Daphni.—
One of those interred there
was the miraculous, the glory of our church,
the holy, the victorious martyr Babylas.

It was him the false god hinted at, him he feared.
As long as he sensed him near he didn't dare
come out with those oracles of his; he was mum.
(The false gods are terrified of our martyrs.)

The impious Julian set himself to work,
exasperated, howling: "Get him up, move him,
oust him, this Babylas, at once.
This is unheard of—Apollo irked!
Get him up, seize him this instant.
Exhume him, take him where you will.
Get rid of him, throw him out. Is this some prank for you?
Apollo's said his temple's to be cleansed."

We took it, we bore the holy relic elsewhere;
We took it, we bore it off with love and honor.

And indeed the temple flourished handsomely.
In no time at all a fire

heated up: a terrible fire:
and the temple was burned, as was Apollo.

The idol was ashes; to be swept out with the trash.

Julian, thwarted, raged and he spread it abroad—
what else could he do—that the fire had
been set by us, the Christians. Let him go on talking.
It hasn't been proved; let him go on talking.
What counts is this: Julian, thwarted, raged.

HIDDEN POEMS: 1884–1923

Beizades to His Beloved

I love you...What if you are daughter to a humble fisherman,
are your eyes for this less bright,
is your hand not whiter than milk,
and your body all erotic joys?
Birth, name, I forget everything completely,
I stand before you your slave, the sovereign's son!

I love you...and when I see you in the flowering valleys
dancing your dance so avidly with the village boys,
I envy them, and grieve at my hard lot,
that I cannot forever be your slave.
Between us fate has raised a terrifying block:
unswayable generations of dragomen and lords!

Dünya Güzeli

The mirror does not lie to me, the sight is true,
there's not another woman as beautiful on earth as me.
My eyes are like gleaming diamonds,
my lips approach the shade of coral,
two rows of pearls adorn my mouth.
My body is graceful, they praise my foot,
all-white hands and neck, silken hair...
       but alas, what good does that do?

Locked as I am inside this hateful harem,
who anywhere on earth beholds my beauty?
Only rival foes cast poisonous glances
my way, the evil eunuchs, and the blood
runs ice in my veins when my odious
husband comes near me. Prophet, Lord over me,
forgive me if my heart cries out in pain,
       Let me be a Christian!

Had I been born a Christian I would be free
to show myself to all, both in the night and day;
and men with wonder, women with envy
would confess, seeing my beauty, with one mind—
That nature will not make another she like me.
Each time I would go forth in an open carriage
the streets of Istanbul would be mobbed
       for everyone to see me.

When, My Friends, I Was in Love

When, my friends, I was in love—
it's many years ago now—
I did not live on the same earth
as other mortals.

I had a lyric
fantasy, and though deceptive,
it granted me happiness
still, alive and ardent.

Whatever the eye saw
it made richer;
my love's nest
appeared a palace.

And the calico dress
she wore, the poor one;
from the start, I swear to you,
it seemed silk to me.

Two poor bracelets
adorned her hands;
for me they were jewels
antique and precious.

On her head she wore
mountain-gathered flowers—
to my eyes what bouquet could
adorn like that?

We always found
our walks together smooth,
and either the earth did not have
brambles then, or else it hid them.

The genius of the rhetors and the sophists
does not persuade me now,
as did one nod of hers
while that time lasted.

When, my friends, I was in love—
it's many years ago now—
I did not live on the same earth
as other mortals.

Nichori

Stranger, when you see a village wherein nature laughs,
and where near every plane tree hides a girl
lovely as a rose—there you should stop;
    you've gotten, stranger, to Nichori.

And when the evening comes, if you go out to walk
and you find before you walnut trees, do not go any further
on your trip along the road. What place can you look for
    elsewhere better than Nichori.

Such freshness elsewhere the world's springs do not have,
the eminence of its hills mountains elsewhere do not have;
and with just the scent of its earth you'll be drunk,
    if you stay even briefly in Nichori.

The greenery you will see there you must not hope
to find in another place. From the mountain look down
to the plains and say how you could not love
    this our little Nichori.

Do not suppose, Oh stranger, that I love exaggerations.
There are many fertile, fruitful places.
They're set apart though, you also must confess it,
    the fruits and flowers in Nichori.

If you wish to enter the Koumariotisa Virgin's
church with me, forgive me if I am
fanatic there. A different grace, I think, belongs
    to prayers in faithful Nichori.

If you can't stay there, stranger, before you set out
you should one Sunday go to the port at Gregory's;
peace you'll see, and youth and joy, and you will understand
    what this place is, our Nichori.

Epic in the Heart

All things with you it seems to me smile affable,
in the mirror of your eyes joy shines back.
Stay, my light, as yet I have not told you even half
those things that grip my heart in passion
and that surge to my lips at just one look from you.
If it is your wish do not speak to me, do not say love's
and adoration's charming words. That you're close here is enough,
that I might say to you I want you, might touch you, breathe
the freshness of the morning that you breathe; and if these
as well you deem excess, that I might see you only!

Stephanos Skilitsis

If souls are immortal, as they tell us,
Stephanos perhaps your soul stays close to us,
and you feel gratified whenever you hear
your name on our lips, and whenever our faithful thoughts
are moved by your dearest memory.

Stephanos, the grave has not separated you from us;
the life we shared was known to everyone.
As little ones we played together; the sorrows of our childhood
and its joys we felt together; and then as young men
we had our first good times together—
until two days ago, O Stephanos, until two days ago, and now
we've led you cold to your final home.

But no. You are among us. The stone at your tomb
will be a thin veil, diaphanous, for us.
And if the gazes of your friends have lost you, their souls
now see you, Stephanos, and later they will have you,
the memories, the hearts of inseparable companions.

Correspondence According to Baudelaire

Aromas inspire me as music,
as rhythm, as beautiful words do,
and I am delighted when in harmonic
verses Baudelaire interprets
all that the marveling soul obscurely
feels in barren emotionality.

"Nature is a temple where living
pillars sometimes utter confused
words. Man passes there
into a dense forest of symbols that intently
observe him with intimate gazes.

"As prolonged sounds merge
from afar in a dark union,
so, in a union vast as darkness
and as light, correspond
the colors, the notes, the aromas.

"There are fragrances fresh
as children's skin; sweet as flutes;
green lands in pasture.

                                    "Others
are rich, corrupt, triumphant;
hymning surges of the spirit and the senses;
holding the pouring out of
infinite things—like the ambrette,
the musk, and the styrax, and the incense."

Believe not only what you see.

The poets' gaze is more acute.

Nature for them is an intimate garden.

In a dark paradise the other
people grope on a difficult road.
And all that shines for them like a spark
sometimes ephemeral on their trek
at night is a feeling, brief, and
random, of magnetic neighborliness—
quick nostalgia, a moment's shudder,
a beautiful dream of dawn,
some undetermined joy flowing suddenly
into the heart, and flying suddenly off.

[Fragments of an untitled poem]

. . . .

one of the dead woman's days, the ghost of a day.
Who this inhuman man was history does not say.
I do not know who the murderer of Ramanakti was.

A fierce-looking Persian satrap reviling an enslaved people
as some relief and retribution for how
he is reviled himself by men with power over him;
or a proud Greek seeing nothing in the world
but his Greece, setting at nought
the tender feeling in a poor barbarian woman
and her pure life's final pure desire.

. . . .

"Nous n'osons plus chanter les roses"

I fearing trite things
silence my many words.
In my heart are written
many poems; and those buried
songs of mine I love.

Oh first, pure, sole freedom
of youth turning toward sex's joy!
Oh the senses' drunken sweetness!
Your divine form makes me fear
the common trope's abuse.

. . . .

Indian Image

The universe has four large gates,
    which four angels guard.
One is the North; the South opposite it;
    and the others West and East.

The gate of the East is of shining pearl;
    and before it a brilliant angel
wears a diamond crown and diamond belt
    and stands on agate ground.

Amethyst, porphyry make up the gate of the South.
    Its guarding angel holds
a magic scepter in hand made of dark sapphire.
    A thick cloud of turquoise
hides his feet.

                    By one bank covered
    with frail red shells
the angel of the West stands and guards
    a gate of precious coral.
He wears a wreath of artificial roses, each rose
    carved in a pure ruby.

The gate of the North built of gold,
    and with a throne before the entrance
. . . .

Pelasgian Image

In the bowels of the earth resides a very ancient Giant.
    His hands number thirty
and thirty his legs. His great neck
    holds up thirty heads
and each has twenty very piercing eyes,
    through which the day
and deepest darkness of the deepest earth shine.
    He is idle and indifferent.
He has countless treasures; great mines
    of silver, diamonds, and gold.
Over his superb wealth, his extraordinary wealth
    with those six hundred eyes
he watches coldly, and sometimes, to get through
    one of his centuries, he counts it.
And then it bores him, he yawns two years,
    and weary falls asleep.
His sleep endures entire centuries;
    his dreams a generation each.
But suddenly, terrified, he wakes. A nightmare—
    offspring of unmastered matter—
disturbed his sleep, in the clouded mirror
    of his apathetic and cold brain
unknown and fearsome phantoms are reflected.
    Then he stretches his huge
limbs and with sixty arms and legs
    he strikes his dome, he kicks. And the earth
shakes at her base; cities collapse,
    and all the rivers flood,
and from the mountains flames, like waves, pour out.
    The ground opens up and closes
and the people tumble and are buried in it.
    But the giant recovers

quickly, and rubbing his enormous eyes
    realizes how vain
that noise, that shaking was
    for the vile shadow of a dream.
He laughs at his cowardice and at all his trembling
    and newly lays him down serene
and the thirty mouths he has smile.

The Hereafter

I believe in the Hereafter. Appetites for the material
or love for the positive do not mislead me.
It isn't a habit but an instinct. The heavenly word

will be added to the incomplete, the otherwise foolish phrase of life.
Rest and reward will succeed activity.
When sight is forever closed to the creation,

the eye will open before the Creator.
A wave of immortal life will flow from each
Gospel of Christ—of indissoluble life.

The Mimiambi of Herodas

For centuries abiding hidden
within the darkness of Egyptian earth,
amid a silence so despairing
injury was done the gracious mimiambi;

but those years have passed,
from the North arrived wise
men, and for the mimiambi entombment
and oblivion ceased. Their humorous tones

have brought back to us again the merriment
of Greek streets and marketplaces;
and together with them we enter the avid
life of a society of intrigue.—

Immediately we're greeted by a masterfully cunning
lady pimp set on corrupting
a wife who's faithful! Mitrichi,
however, knows how virtue is protected.

Next we see another obscene type
who presides over an establishment
and who maniacally accuses a man from Phrygia
of injury to—a school of girls.

Two gaggling sorts, elegant ladies
pay a visit to Asklepios;
their fiercest talk cheers
the temple mightily.

With the good Mitro
we enter a grand shop of leather goods.
Handsome things lie about abundantly here,
here the latest fashion's to be found.

But how many were missing from the papyri;
how often the light and ironic iambs
were food for foul silk-devouring worms!
Oh unlucky Herodas, created
to gibe, made for gaiety,
how sorely wounded he has come to us!

Blue Eyes

These vibrant spheres of light were not made
    for scorn, oh beautiful Circassian girl.
Not wrath's, but joy's and passion's lamps,
      pleasure's lavish donors,
        promise of sweetness in fleshly delight.

Had they been made for stern resolve against an ardent heart
    and to wreck havoc;
had they been sent to earth from a god in wrath;
    they would have had

some other form, and the mild dome of skies
    would not have given them its tender hue at all,
the sun who pours out bounty would never have consented
      that fire or that sheen be granted them
      from his flaming erotic body.

The Four Walls of My Room

....

I know that they're all modest,
and that other ornaments
were due my friends, more distinguished
and more numerous, larger also.

But what do these words mean?
My walls have better manners;
and they don't love me for my gifts.
They are not like people.

Besides, they know that my things
will last only a moment
even for me. My joys and my sorrows
and everything I have here below

will pass quickly. The old
walls are indifferent to such gifts.
They are long-lived and from my
short life do not require anything.

Alexandrian Merchant

He sold rotten barley at a high price.
This Rome is the kingdom of
well-turned profit. Plus, I've arrived in April:
in April I depart. I've lost no time.

The ocean seems somewhat tiresome to me;
a great cloud blocks the sun.
What of it? To me every rock is a seashell,
every sea like any level field.

I do not fear the great air's sloping breaths.
I laugh at storms and wrecks at sea.
Broad-laned Alexandria

will receive me safely.... Friends there, watch out!
keep your distance from the jug! What a reckless feast he makes!
After the voyage the soul thirsts for the wines of Samos.

The Hospitality of Lagides

Ptolemy Philopator receives
the sophist Medon royally—
researcher of the soul's powers.
The king exults in the foreigner.

At another time in corrupting
Rome, the sophist, poor, had offered his opus
to a high potentate. From him, though:
"Receive of me this mina and depart. Drivel bores me."

"Oh insolence, insolence! Studying the infinite
I charactered all feeling, incandescent,
my heart entire in this

papyrus...." But, despising the dictator,
he broke off his epic assertions.—
Honor to Ptolemy Philopator.

In the Cemetery

When memory directs
your footsteps to the cemetery,
in reverence worship
the sacred mystery in our dark future.
Lift up your mind to the Lord.
Before you
the narrow bed of boundless sleep
lies under the mercy of Jesus.

Our beloved religion
preserves our graves in modesty.
The gifts and victims of the pagans
and their pomp do not please it.
Without votive offerings, inane,
of gold,
the narrowest bed of boundless sleep
lies under the mercy of Jesus.

Priam's Speeding Forth at Night

Pain in Ilium and wailing.
                    The earth
at Troy in bitter hopelessness and dread
weeps for Priam's great son Hector.

The loud keening echoes, heavily.
                    No soul
is left in Troy who is not mourning,
who turns his mind away from Hector.

But it is vain, fruitless
                    great
keening in a city suffering, wracked;
adverse destiny goes deaf.

Priam, hating what is fruitless,
                    takes
gold out of the treasury; he adds
cauldrons, carpets, and soldiers' cloaks; and

chitons moreover, tripods, a pile of bright
                    peplums,
plus whatever other offerings he finds handy,
and heaps them on his chariot.

He wants, with ransom, from the terrible
                    foe,
to regain the body of his child,
and do it honor with a reverential funeral.

He leaves in the silent night.
                    He says
little. He thinks now only
that his chariot must run swiftly, swiftly.

The road stretches dark.
                    Pitying
the wind laments and wails.
A frightful raven cries out far off, harsh.

Here, the barking of a dog is heard;
                    there,
whisper-like, swift-footed, passed a hare.
The king spurs, spurs the horses on.

The shadows of the plain awaken, stormy
                    shadows,
and they wonder for what cause in such haste
the son of Dardanus flies so toward the ships

of the murdering Argives and uncouth
                    Achaians.
The king, however, pays no attention to all that;
it is enough that his chariot runs swiftly, swiftly.

Epitaph

Stranger, beside the Ganges I lie, a man
from Samos. On this thrice-barbarous earth
I lived a life of pain, of toil, of lamentation.
This grave beside the river

encloses many griefs. Insatiable longing
for gold pushed me into cursed trade.
A storm cast me on the Indian coast
and I was sold then as a slave. Up to old age

I more than toiled, I gasped to work—
deprived of a Greek voice, and far
from the shores of Samos. So now nothing horrible

afflicts me, nor do I make my way to Hades mourning.
There I will be among compatriots.
And through the future I will speak in Greek.

A Displeased Viewer

"I'm leaving, I'm leaving. Do not detain me.
I'm the victim of boredom and disgust."
"But stay a little for Menander's sake. It's a pity
to deprive yourself of so much." "You abuse me, lout.

"Are these maunderings Menander's,
these worthless verses and childish verbs?
Let me leave the theater at once
and make my way, delivered, to my proper place.

"The air of Rome has corrupted you completely.
Instead of condemning, you give a coward's praise,
you applaud the barbarian—what's he called?

"Gavrentios, Terence?—one
good only in the Latin, the Atellan theaters,
who desires our Menander's glory."

To Jerusalem

[a]
Now they've gotten to Jerusalem.
Passion, avarice, and ambition
and the suspect pride of knights
from their souls they have renounced.

Now they've gotten to Jerusalem.
In their ecstasy and in their fixed devotion
they've forgotten their quarrels with the Greeks,
they've forgotten their hatred for the Turks.

Now they've gotten to Jerusalem.
And the unvanquished Crusaders,
the formerly intrepid and audacious,
are cowardly and nervous, they are not able
to advance, they tremble as do little children
and as little children do they weep, all of them weep,
beholding the walls of Jerusalem.

[b]
Now they've come before Jerusalem.
Passion, avarice, and ambition,
likewise their suspect pride,
they've discharged from their hearts at once.

Now they've come before Jerusalem.
In their ecstasy and their fixed devotion
they've forgotten their quarrels with the Greeks,
they've forgotten hatred of the Turks.

Now they've come before Jerusalem.
And the unvanquished and intrepid Crusaders,

those violent in each of their procedures and assaults,
are cowardly and nervous and not able
to advance; they tremble like little children,
and like little children cry, all cry,
beholding the walls of Jerusalem.

A Second Odyssey

Dante, *Inferno*, Canto XXVI
Tennyson, "Ulysses"

A second Odyssey, long again,
equal, it may be, to the first. But without
Homer, alas, without hexameters.

The roof where he was father was small,
the city where he was father was small,
and the whole of his Ithaca was small.

The affection of Telemachus, the faith
of Penelope, the father's old age,
his old friends, the devoted
subjects' love,
the providential comfort of home
came like rays of happiness
to the heart of the seafarer.

And like rays they fastened.

            The thirst
the sea gives woke in him.
He hated dry land's air.
The ghosts of the Hesperides
troubled his sleep at night.
Nostalgia for the voyage hurt
him everywhere, and for morning
arrivals in harbors that you enter,
with such joy, for the first time.

The affection of Telemachus, the faith
of Penelope, the father's old age,

his old friends, the devoted
subjects' love,
and the peace and repose
of home bored him.

               And he left.

Gradually, while the shores of Ithaca
vanished in the way before him
and he set all sails west,
to Iberia, to the Pillars of Hercules,—
far from every Achaian sea,—
he felt he was alive again, that
he had cast aside the heavy bonds
of known, of household things.
And his adventuring heart
exulted in a cold and vacant love.

One Who Has Failed

For one who has failed, one brought low
how difficult it is to learn poverty's
new language, its new manners.

How will he go to vile houses of strangers!—
what will his heart be as he walks the street
and when he finds himself before the door where will he find
the strength to touch the bell.
For the base need of bread
and shelter, how will he offer thanks!
How will he meet the cold eyes
that will show him he's a burden!
How will the lips that are proud now
begin to speak with humility;
and how will the head, ascendant, bow!
How will he hear the phrases that
lacerate, word by word, the ears—and despite that
you must feign that you sense none of this
as if you are a simple soul and do not notice things.

The Pawn

Frequently, while I watch people playing chess,
my eyes follow one pawn
that little by little finds his way
and safely makes it to the last line.
He goes with such a will to the edge
that you think surely they'll start here,
his pleasures and rewards.
On the road he meets with many hardships.
Infantries cast spears obliquely at him;
fortresses strike him with their broad
lines; within their two squares
swift horsemen seek artfully
for ways to block him;
and here and there with a cornering threat
into his road comes some pawn
sent from the enemy camp.

But he escapes from all the dangers
and makes it to the last line.

How triumphantly he makes it to this place,
to the threatening last line;
how willingly he comes up to his death!

Because here the Pawn will perish
and his pains were all for this alone.
For the queen, who will save us,
to resurrect her from the tomb
he came to fall down into chess's Hades.

Terror

In the night, my Lord Jesus,
  guard my mind and soul for me
    when Beings and Things that have no name
  start to walk around me and with feet
that are not flesh run all through my room
and make a circle round my bed to look at me—
    and watch me as though they know me,
as though mute laughter burst from them that they could scare me
  now.

  I know it, yes, they wait for me
    as though they had in mind abominable times
in which I maybe crawled along with them—in the darkness
with those beings and those things, disoriented.
    Frenzy drives their longing for that past to come again.
    But it will never come back now; since I'm one saved,
      baptized in the name of Christ.

    I tremble in the evening when I sense
      when I know that deep in the darkness
        eyes are fixed on me....
  Hide me from their sight, my Lord.
And while they speak or threaten, let no single
cast-out word of theirs reach my ears,
    lest it happen that they bring into my soul
some recollection of hideous, hidden things they know.

In the House of the Soul

Deeper, at the deepest, in the House of the Soul,
Where they come and go and sit around the fire,
The Passions with their women's faces.
      —Rodenbach

Within the House of the Soul the Passions go about—
    comely women dressed in silk,
  each head adorned with sapphires.
From the door of the house even to its depths
they hold sway in every hall. In the grandest—
    on the nights their blood runs hot—
they dance and drink, their hair unbound.

  Outside the halls, pale and poorly dressed
    in clothes of former days,
  the Virtues go about and hear with bitterness
the revels that the drunken hetaerae enjoy.
On windows' panes the faces press
    contemplative, silent, and they watch
the lights, the jewels, and the flowers of the dance.

Rain

. . . .
a small garden
has two slim trees;
and there the water makes
the countryside a parody—
coming in where branches
have no secrets;
watering roots
that have unhealthy sap;
running in the foliage
that, tied with threads
prosaic and melancholy,
hangs in the windows;
and cleaning wasted plants
placed in windows
row on row in pots
by a sensible housewife.

Rain, which the little children
watch joyfully
from within a warm room,
clapping hands and jumping more
the more the water
grows and falls.
Rain, which old men hear
with sullen patience,
heavy bored;
because they instinctively
bear no love at all
to earth made wet, to shadows.

Rain, rain—ceaseless
headlong the rain goes on.

But now I can't see.
The window glass
is blurred with so much water.
On its surface
scattered drops
run, glide, and spread
and rise and fall
and each one stains
and each one clouds.
And at last the road,
dazzled dim, shows only barely,
as, in the frosting rain,
the houses and the coaches do.

La Jeunesse blanche

Our dearest, our white youth,
ah our white, our perfectly white youth,
boundless, and so much for a little while,
which, above us, like an archangel, opens wings!...
It exhausts itself completely, it loves everything;
and it melts and faints in horizons of white.
Ah, it goes there and is lost in horizons of white,
it goes forever.

Forever, no. It will return,
it will come back, it will return again.
With its pure limbs, its pure grace,
our white youth will come to hold us.
With its pure hands it will take us up,
and with a light shroud brought forth from its whiteness,
with a perfectly white shroud brought forth from its whiteness
it will cover us.

Distinguishing Marks

Other lands bear other fruits and bounty.
The horse shows the Thessalian... The fruit
of this city, though, is word and man.
    —Himerios

Every land has its distinguishing marks.
Horses and horsemanship are peculiar to the Thessalian;
    the hour of war marks out
    the Spartan; Media has

    choice food at table;
the hair shows a Celt, the beard an Assyrian.
    But Athens as its distinction
    has Man and the Word.

Eternity

The Indian king Arjuna, humane and mild,
hated slaughter. He never waged war.
But the fearful war god was displeased—
(his glory was diminished, his temples emptied)—
and in a mighty rage he entered the palace of Arjuna.
The king was afraid and said: "Great God,
forgive me if I cannot take a human life!"
With contempt the god answered: "You think
yourself more just than I? Don't be fooled by words.
Not one life is taken. Know that no one
was ever born, nor does anyone die."

Confusion

My soul is, in the middle of the night,
confused and paralyzed. Outside,
    outside itself its life occurs.

And it awaits the unlikely dawn.
And I wait, both perishing and bored.
    I too, within it or beside it.

Salome

Upon a golden tray Salome brings
   the head of John the Baptist
     to the young Greek sophist
who's shown himself indifferent to love.

"Salome," replies the youth,
   "I wanted them to bring your head to me."
     He speaks this way in jest.
And the next day one of her servants comes running

carrying the head of the Beloved
   all blond upon a golden tray.
     But the sophist, studying, had forgotten
his desire of the day before.

He sees the blood dripping and is disgusted.
   He orders that bloody thing
     to be taken up away from him, and continues
reading the dialogues of Plato.

Chaldaic Image

Before the god Ea fashioned humankind, the earth
      was full of the odious offspring
of Apsu—who had abysses with no limit for a body—
      and of Mummus Tamat, watery chaos.
Warriors existed then with vultures' bodies;
      Nations with human bodies
and raven heads; human-headed
      races of bulls, tall and massive;
and dogs that barked through night and day, who had
      four bodies and tails
of fish.—The god Ea and our other gods
      exterminated the whole lot entirely
before placing humankind in Paradise
      (from where, alas, how wretchedly it's fallen).

Julian at the Mysteries

But when he found himself in darkness,
in the earth's frightening depths,
accompanied by infidel Greeks,
and saw bodiless shapes emerging
in bursts of glory and blazing lights before him,
the young man was scared for a moment,
and an instinct from his reverent years
returned, and he crossed himself.
Instantly the shapes disappeared;
the glories vanished—the lights went out.
The Greeks cast covert looks one to another.
And the young man said; "Did you see the miracle?
My beloved companions, I'm frightened.
I'm frightened, my friends, I want to leave.
Didn't you see how the demons vanished at once
when they saw I was making
the holy sign of the cross?"
The Greeks' laughter rang out contemptuous, grand;
"It's shameful, it shames you to speak those words
to us, sophists and philosophers.
You can say things like that to
the Bishop of Nicomedia, and to his priests, if you like.
Before you appeared the preeminent gods
of our glorious Greece.
And if they left, don't think at all
that they were afraid of a gesture.
Only that when they saw you making
that utterly servile, boorish sign
their noble nature was disgusted
and they left, and did so despising you."
That's how they answered him, and from his
holy and blessed fear
the simpleton recovered,
believing the words of the Greeks, godless.

The Cat

The cat provokes antipathy in common men.
Magnetic and secretive, she wearies
    their superficial minds; and on her charming ways
      they place no value. [   ]
    [   ]
    [   ]

But the cat's soul is in her pride.
Her blood and nerves are freedom.
    Never are her glances humble.
      In her passion for everything hidden,
  in her cleanliness, her calmness
  and beautiful stance, the restraint

she shows, how fine a sense of purity
is found. When cats dream or sleep
    a coldness, visionary, gathers all around them.
    Perhaps they've been encircled from afar

by ghosts of ancient times. Perhaps the vision
guides them back to Bubastis; where their sanctuaries
    were, where Ramses traveled once to worship them,
    where, to the priests, their motions all were omens.

The Bank of the Future

      To keep my difficult life safe
I will draw very few advances
from the Bank of the Future.

      I doubt it has much capital.
And I've begun to fear that in the first crisis
it suddenly will stop its payments.

What Cannot Be

There still exists one blessed joy
one comfort in this sorrow.
How many throngs of worthless days are absent
in this consummation, how many boring griefs are absent!

A poet said; "Beloved
is that music given not to sound."
And I deem most exceptional
that life not given to be lived.

Addition

Whether I am happy or unhappy I do not question.
But I do, with joy, keep one thing in mind—
that in the great addition (their addition that I hate)
that has so many numbers, I am not one
of all the many numbers there. In the total sum
I have not been numbered. And for me that joy suffices.

Bouquets

Absinthe, datura, and vigna,
aconite, hellebore, and hemlock—
all the bitter ones and poisons—
will give their leaves and fearsome blossoms
that the great bouquets might be made
which will lie on the shining altar—
ah, the gleaming altar of Malachite—
stone of the Passion fearsome, most beautiful.

Lohengrin

The good king pities Elsa
and turns to the Herald of the Court.

The Herald summons, and the bugles sound.

Oh King, I beseech you once more,
once more let the Herald summon.

Again the Herald summons.

            I entreat you,
I fall at your feet. Have pity on me, have pity.
He's far away, very far away, he does not hear.
For one last time let the Herald
summon now. Perhaps he will appear.

            The Herald
calls anew his summons.

       And soon something
white shone on the horizon.
It has appeared, it has appeared—it is the swan.

Oh our misfortune, oh misfortune, when
the king feels pity, and to his Herald
turns mechanically, without much hope.
And the Herald summons and the bugles sound.
    And again he summons and the bugles sound;
    And again he summons and the bugles sound;
    but Lohengrin never comes to him.

And yet faith would still keep watch, inviolate.

Suspicion

And who will speak of the worst.
(That were better left untold.)
Who will come to tell us (Let us not heed him.
Let us not heed him. They will have deceived him.)
the unjust accusation; and afterwards
the challenge, then again the challenge from the Herald,
the glorious entrance of Lohengrin—
swan, and magic sword, and holy grail—
and at long last his duel,
in which Telramund was victor over him.

Death of a General

Death extends his hand
and touches the brow of a glorious general.
In the evening the paper breaks the news.
The sick one's house swarms with a great crowd.

Pains have paralyzed the man,
his limbs and tongue. He gazes about,
and for a long time looks intently at familiar objects.
Tranquil, he remembers the old heroes.

Outwardly—silence and immobility covered him.
Within—life's envy rotted him, as did cowardice,
voluptuous leprosy, moronic obstinacy, rage, malice.

He groans heavily.—He's died.—Lament fills every civic
voice; "His death's destroyed our city!
Virtue, alas, had died along with him!"

The Intervention of the Gods

Heartily know,

...

The gods arrive.
    —Emerson

REMONIN: He will disappear at the crucial
   moment; the gods will intervene.
Mme DE RUMIÈRES: As in the ancient tragedies?
      (act 2, scene 1)
Mme DE RUMIÈRES: What is it?
REMONIN: The Gods have arrived.
      (act 5, scene 10)
    —Alexandre Dumas fils, *L'Étrangère*

This will happen now, and subsequently that;
and later on, in one or two years (in my judgment),
actions will be of this or that sort, as will manners.
We will not concern ourselves with distant times to come.
We'll try for the best.
And the more we try, the more we'll spoil,
complicate matters, until we find ourselves
in utter confusion. And then we will stop.
It will be time for the gods to arrive.
The gods always come. They will descend
from their machines, and some they will save,
others they'll violently, suddenly
dispatch; and when they bring some order
they will withdraw.—And then this one will do that thing,
and that one do another; and in time the rest
will do theirs. And then we will start again.

242

King Claudius

My mind goes to places far away.
I walk the streets of Elsinore,
I wander in the square and remember
the story, pitiful in the extreme,
of that luckless king,
who was killed by his nephew
because of purely imagined suspicions.

In all the houses of the poor,
secretly (because they feared Fortinbras)
he was wept for. He was serene and
gentle; and he loved peace
(the place had suffered much
from its former ruler's wars).
He behaved nobly with everyone,
grand and humble. He hated
arbitrary arrogance, and sought counsel
in his kingdom's affairs always
from serious and experienced persons.

What cause his nephew had to kill him
they could never say for sure.
He suspected him of murder.
The basis of his suspicion was that
one night while walking high atop
one of the ancient battlements,
he thought he saw a ghost,
a ghost with whom he spoke.
And supposedly he heard from the ghost
some accusations concerning the king.

It must have been a flash of fantasy
of course, and an optical illusion.

(The prince was nervous in the extreme.
While he was studying in Wittenberg
many of his fellow students thought him a maniac.)

A few days later he went
to his mother's to talk
over some familial concerns. And suddenly,
while he was talking, he went berserk
and started to shriek, and to shout
that the ghost was there in front of him.
But his mother didn't see a thing.

And the same day he killed
an old courtier for no reason.
As the prince was due to go
to England in a day or two,
the king seized the moment and sent him off at once,
in order to save him.
But the people were so outraged
by the horrendous murder
that rebels rose up
and sought to smash
the palace gates, at their side
the slain man's son, the Lord Laertes
(a brave young man, ambitious as well;
in the melee "Long Live King Laertes"
was called out by some of his friends).

After all that, when the place had calmed down
and the king lay in his grave,
killed by his nephew
(the prince didn't go to England;
on the way he jumped ship),
a certain Horatio showed up
and tried, with some explanatory tales,

to vindicate the prince.
He said the trip to England
had been a secret plot, and that an order
had been given to kill the prince there.
(This, however, was never clearly proved.)
He spoke as well of poisoned wine,
poisoned by the king.
Laertes also, it's true, said this.
But couldn't he have lied? Couldn't he have erred?
And when did he say it? When, wounded,
he was dying, and his mind was reeling,
and he seemed to be raving.
As for the poisoned weapons,
it was shown later that
the king hadn't applied the poison at all,
Laertes applied it himself.
But Horatio, when he needed to,
brought in the ghost as evidence.
The ghost said this, said that!
The ghost did this and that!

All that, although they listened while he spoke,
caused most people to think
sadly of their poor king
who, amid phantoms and fairy tales,
had been unjustly killed, had made his exit.

But Fortinbras, who had benefited
and easily seized power,
gave great weight and full attention
to the words of Horatio.

The Naval Battle

We were annihilated there in Salamis.
Let us say woe, woe, woe, woe, woe, woe.
Ecbatana, Susa, and Persepolis
are ours—the most beautiful places.
What were we seeking there in Salamis
that we hauled in fleets and did battle at sea.
Now we will go back to our Ecbatana,
we will go to our Persepolis, and to Susa.
We'll go, but we will not enjoy them as at first.
Alas, alas; this naval battle,
why should it occur, what demands it.
Alas, alas; what obliges us
to rise up, to abandon everything
and go there to battle so vilely at sea.
Why must it be like this: as soon as one
possesses the renowned Ecbatana, Susa,
and Persepolis, he assembles a fleet immediately,
and goes out to do battle with the Greeks at sea.
Ah yes, of course; we need not say another word:
alas, alas, alas.
Ah yes, indeed; what more is left for us to say:
woe, woe, woe, woe, woe, woe.

When the Watchman Saw the Light

Winter, summer, on the roof of Atreus's house
the watchman sat and looked out.
Now he tells a joyous thing. Far away he's seen
a fire lit. And he's glad; and his toil likewise ceases.
It's hard labor, night and day,
in heat and cold, looking over
to Arachnaion for fire. Now it's shone,
the longed for signal. When satisfaction
arrives, it offers a smaller joy
than one expected. Nonetheless, this much
has been plainly gained: we're saved
from hope and expectation. Many things
will befall the house of Atreus. Without being wise
anyone can infer this now that the watchman
has seen the light. Therefore, no hyperbole.
The light is good; and those who come are good;
and their words and deeds are also good.
And let us wish that all ends justly.
But Argos can manage without the house of Atreus.
Houses are not eternal.
Much, surely, will be said by many. Let us listen.
But the Indispensable, the Sole, the Mighty—
that talk will not fool us.
Indispensable, sole, mighty—
instantly one can always find another of that sort.

The Enemies

Three sophists came to greet the Consul.
The Consul seated them close to him.
He spoke to them politely. And later, jokingly,
he told them to take care. "Fame makes
enviers of men. Rivals write. You have enemies."
One of the three answered with serious words.

"Our contemporary enemies will never harm us.
Our enemies will come later, the new sophists.
When we, extremely old, will lie piteously in bed;
and when some of us will have entered Hades. Today's
words and our works will seem odd (and comical
perhaps) because the enemies will change
sophistries, styles, and rankings. In the same way as I,
and as those others, who refashioned the past so much.
Whatever we represented as lovely and correct
the enemies will prove to be inane and extravagant,
saying the same things again differently (without great effort).
As we too said the old words in another manner."

Artificial Flowers

I don't want real narcissi—nor do I like
    lilies, or real roses.
They make the trite, the common gardens pretty. Their flesh
    embitters me, tires and grieves me—
        I am weary of their perishable beauties.

Give me artificial flowers—flowers of china and of metal—
which do not wither and do not rot, with forms that do not age.
    Flowers from the superb gardens of another place,
    where Theories, and Rhythms, and Learning dwell.

I love flowers fashioned of glass or of gold,
    faithful gifts of a faithful Art;
with colors dyed more beautiful than nature's,
    worked in nacre and enamel,
        with ideal leaves and branches.

They draw their grace from wise and purest Taste;
they did not grow in filth of earth or mud.
    If they have no aroma, we'll pour them fragrance,
    we'll burn before them myrrh of sentiment.

Becoming Stronger

Whoever desires to strengthen his spirit,
let him leave behind respect, submission.
He will keep certain laws,
but for the most part he will break
both laws and customs, and leave
the acceptable, inadequate straight way behind.
He will be taught much by the pleasures of the flesh.
He will not fear the catastrophic deed;
half the house must be demolished.
So he will evolve virtuously in wisdom.

September 1903

At least let me now beguile myself with false hopes;
and so not notice my empty life.

And so many times I was so close.
And how I froze, how I recoiled, afraid;
why stop, with my lips closed;
and have my empty life weep inside me,
and my longing put on mourning black?

To be close so many times
to the erotic eyes, the lips,
to the dreamsought, the beloved body.
To be close so many times.

December 1903

And if I am unable to utter my erotic life—
if I do not speak of your hair, of those lips, those eyes;
still, your face, that I hold in my soul,
the sound of your voice, that I hold in my mind,
the days of September that dawn in my dreams,
fashion and color my words and phrases,
whatever theme I turn to, whatever thought I tell.

January 1904

Ah this January's nights,
in which I sit and with the mind create again
those moments and then meet you,
and hear our last words and hear the first.

This January's nights without hope,
when the vision goes, leaving me alone.
How fast it goes, dissolves—
gone are the trees, gone are the streets, gone the houses,
gone the lights;
it fades and is lost, your erotic form.

On the Stairs

As I was going down that defiled staircase,
you were entering at the door, and for one moment
I saw your face, unknown, and you saw me.
Just after that I hid so you would not see me again, and you
went past quickly, hiding your face,
and you fled hard into that defiled house
where you would not find pleasure, as I did not.

And yet the body's love you wanted I had to give to you;
the body's love I wanted—your eyes told me that,
tired and suspicious—you had to give to me.
Our bodies searching sensed and asked for one another;
our blood and skin understood.

But we hid ourselves, the two of us, trembling afraid.

At the Theater

I got bored with watching the stage,
and raised my eyes to the boxes.
And in one box I saw you
with your strange beauty, and depraved youth.
And instantly everything came back to mind,
all they'd said of you to me that afternoon;
both contemplation and my body thrilled.
And as, spellbound, I beheld
your weary beauty, your weary youth,
your perfectly chosen clothes,
in revery I pictured you
as they'd told me of you in the afternoon.

Poseidonians

Those Poseidonians of the Tyrrhenean Gulf, despite their Greek origin,
made perfect barbarians of themselves, becoming Tyrrheneans or Romans,
and changing their speech, their many customs, except for one Greek
holiday, one they observe even now, on which they gather and remember
their ancient names and customs, bewailing it all for each other and
departing in tears.
    —Athenaios

The Poseidonians forgot the Greek language,
mixed in for so many centuries
with Tyrrheneans, and with Italiotes, and other foreigners.
The one ancestral remnant left to them
was a Greek holiday, with beautiful rites,
with lyres and flutes, with contests and coronals.
And habitually, toward the holiday's end,
they would tell each other about their ancient customs,
and would say the Greek names once more,
which precious few barely understood.
And their holiday always ended melancholy.
Because they remembered they too were Greeks—
they too had been Greeks in Italy;
and how they'd fallen now, how they'd changed,
living and speaking barbarically,
withdrawn—oh the calamity!—from Hellenism.

The End of Antony

But when he heard the women crying
and keening over his ruin,
the mistress with eastern gestures,
and the servants with their barbarically disfigured Greek,
the pride in his soul
rose up, revulsion flared in his Italian blood,
and everything seemed foreign and inane to him
that up till then he had worshiped blindly—
all of his passionate Alexandrian life—
and he said, "They must not cry for him. None of that was fitting.
But they should sing his praise instead,
that he had been a magnificent ruler,
that he had amassed abundant treasure and goods.
And if he's fallen now, he hasn't fallen humbly,
but as a Roman by a Roman overcome."

27 June 1906, 2 P.M.

When the Christians brought him out to hang him,
the seventeen-year-old, the innocent boy,
his mother, who near the gallows
crawled and beat herself on the scattered earth,
under the fierce noonday sun,
howled, and sometimes cried out like a wolf, like a wild beast;
exhausted sometimes the mother-martyr keened,
"Only seventeen, the years you've lived for me, my boy."
And when they took him up the gallows steps
and over him knotted the rope and strangled him,
the seventeen-year-old, the innocent boy,
and there hung in the void, pitiable,
convulsed in black anguish,
the beautifully made ephebic body,
the mother-martyr rocked herself on the scattered earth
and now no longer keened for years;
"Only seventeen days" was her dirge,
"only seventeen days, my joy, my pride with you, my boy."

Hidden Things

From all I did and all I said
let no one try to find out who I was.
An obstacle stood there and transfigured
the actions and demeanor of my life.
An obstacle stood there and stopped me
many times when I'd start out to speak.
My most unnoticed actions
and my most covert written work—
from these alone will others know me.
It may, though, not be worth their exerting such elaborate
attention and taking so much care to find me out.
After this—in a more perfect society—
another man made as I was
will certainly appear and will act freely.

On Hearing of Love

On hearing of powerful love, tremble, and feel it
like an aesthete. But then, made happy,
remember how many things your imagination fashioned for you;
    those
first; and next the others—slighter—that you've
experienced and enjoyed in your life, those truer and tangible.—
Of such loves you were not deprived.

"The Rest I Will Tell to Those Below in Hades"

"Indeed," said the proconsul, closing the book, "this
verse is beautiful and quite correct;
Sophocles wrote it deep in philosophic reverie.
How many things we'll say there, how many things we'll say there.
And how different we'll appear.
What we, like sleepless guards, hold fast here,
wounds and secrets that we shut away inside ourselves,
with rigor, anguish every day,
we'll speak of freely there, and clearly."

"Add," said the sophist, half-smiling,
"if that's the talk down there, if they care at all anymore."

So

In this obscene photograph covertly
(so no policeman would see) sold in the street,
in this whorish photograph,
how did such a face appear,
the face one dreams; how did you turn up here.

Who knows what a degrading, vulgar life you must live;
how horrible the surroundings must have been
when you posed for them to photograph you;
how base a soul yours must be.
All that, and more, aside, for me you stay
the face one dreams, the form
fashioned for, given for sensual Greek joy—
so you stay for me and so my poetry declares you.

Return from Greece

So, we've almost arrived, Hermippos.
Day after tomorrow, I think; so said the captain.
At least we're sailing on our own sea;
waters of Cyprus, of Syria, and of Egypt,
beloved waters of our native lands.
Why so silent? Ask your heart,
didn't you also feel happier
the farther we got from Greece? Can fooling ourselves pay?—
that wouldn't be exactly Greek.

Now let's admit the truth;
we too are Greeks—what else are we?—
but our inclinations and our feelings come from Asia,
inclinations and feelings
startling at times to Hellenism.

It does not befit us, Hermippos, philosophers that we are,
to be like some of our lesser kings
(remember how we laughed at them
when they visited our classes)
through whose exteriors, made ostentatiously
Greek, and (what a word!) Macedonian,
a bit of Arabia slips out at times,
a bit of Media that cannot be snatched back,
and the poor things, what laughable wiles
their efforts to keep it all unobserved.

Ah no, such things do not befit us.
Such mincing will not do for Greeks like us.
Let's not be ashamed of the blood of Syria and of Egypt
that flows through our veins,
let us do it honor, let us exult in it.

Exiles

And yet it's Alexandria. Should you walk a little
on the straight road that ends at the Hippodrome,
you'll see palaces and monuments, and marvel.
However it's been marred in wars,
however it's been reduced, it stays a wonderful city.
And then with excursions and with books,
and with diverse studies the time goes by.
In the evenings we meet by the shore,
we five (under names that all have been
assumed, of course) together with some of those
few Greeks who have stayed in the city.
Sometimes we discuss church affairs (they're
more like Romans here), sometimes literature.
Two days ago we read verses by Nonnos.
What images, what rhythms, what language, what harmony.
Enthused, we all admired the Panopolitan.
The days pass by like this, and the sojourn
is not unpleasant, because, of course,
there's no idea of its being everlasting.
We've had good news, and whether
something happens for us now in Smyrna, or in April
our friends set out from Epiros, our plans
are working out, and we'll overthrow Basil easily.
And then finally our turn will also come.

Theophilos Palaiologos

This is the last year. He is the last
emperor of the Greeks. And, alas,
how grievously those at his side speak.
In his desperation, in his pain,
Kyr Theophilos Palaiologos
says, "I'd rather die than live."

Ah, Kyr Theophilos Palaiologos,
how much of our race's thwarted hope, and how much exhaustion
(how much weariness from injustices and persecution)
your five tragic words contained.

And I Reclined and Lay on their Beds

When I came into pleasure's house,
I didn't stay in the spacious room where they celebrate,
with somewhat decent manners, acknowledged loves.

I went to the hidden rooms
and I reclined and lay on their beds.

I went to the hidden rooms
which they're ashamed to even name.
But not shameful to me—for then
what kind of poet and what kind of artist would I be?
I'd sooner live a hermit. It would be more consonant,
far more consonant with my poetry,
than for me to enjoy myself in the commonplace, the spacious room.

Half an Hour

I never had you, nor will I have you
ever, I suppose. A few words, a drawing
near as in the bar two days ago, and nothing more.
It is, I don't claim otherwise, something to regret. But we,
Art's people, by intensity of mind,
and then naturally for just a little while, sometimes create
pleasure whose effects seem almost bodily, substantial.
In that way, in the bar two days ago—merciful
alcohol helping things along as well—
I had a perfectly erotic half an hour.
And it seems to me you understood,
and purposely remained a little longer.
That was very necessary. Because
for all the imagination, for all the magic spirit of the wine,
I needed to see your lips as well,
I needed to have your body close to me.

House with a Garden

I'd like to have a country house
with a very large garden—not so much
for the flowers, for the trees, and the greenery
(they too must certainly be present; they're exceedingly lovely)
but so that I can have animals. Ah, to have animals!
At the least, seven cats—two of them jet-black,
and two all white as snow, for the contrast.
An estimable parrot, so I can listen to him
saying things with emphasis and conviction.
As for dogs, I believe three would be enough for me.
I'd also want two horses (little horses are good).
And without fail three, four of those distinguished,
those agreeable animals, the donkeys,
to sit there idly, their heads one proud pleasure.

A Great Feast at the Home of Sosibios

Beautiful, my afternoon was very
beautiful. The oar caresses, just so
lightly touches, the sweetly smoothed Alexandrian sea.
One needs some respite of this kind: they are weighty, the fruits of
  labor.
Let's also take the innocent and mild view of things, at times.
But evening's come, unfortunately. And there, I've drunk all the wine,
not a drop's left in my bottle.
It's time for us to turn, alas, to other things.
A glorious house (the eminent Sosibios and his
good wife; let's say it that way) bids us feast in it.
We've got to go to our cabals again—
take up, once more, our tiresome politics.

Simeon

Yes, I know his new poems;
Beirut's enthusiastic over them.
I'll study them some other day.
Today I can't, because I am, to some degree, unsettled.

Certainly he is more learned in Greek than Libanius.
But better than Meleager? I don't believe so.

Ah Mebis, no Libanius! and no books!
and no trivialities! . . . . Mebis, yesterday I stood—
fortune led me there—below Simeon's pillar.

I thrust myself in among the Christians
who were praying and worshiping in silence,
bowing there in reverence; not being a Christian,
I lacked their spiritual peace—
and I trembled all over and suffered;
I was shattered, unnerved, and aghast.

Ah, don't smile; for thirty-five years, think of it—
winter, summer, daytime, night, for thirty-five
years he's been living, martyring himself, atop a pillar.
Before we were born—I'm twenty-nine years old,
you are, I think, younger than I am—
before we were born, imagine it,
Simeon climbed up that pillar
and since that time has stayed there facing God.

I have no head for work today.—
Still you'd better say this much to them, Mebis,
that, whatever the other Sophists may say,
I acknowledge Lamon
as Syria's chief poet.

The Bandaged Shoulder

He said he'd knocked against a wall, or that he'd fallen.
Most likely, though, some other cause
explained the wounded, bandaged shoulder.

With a slightly violent motion,
one made to take down from a shelf
some photographs he wanted to look at closely,
the bandage opened and a little blood spilled.

I bound the shoulder tight again, and at the binding
lingered some; since it didn't hurt him,
and because I liked seeing the blood. It was something
belonging to my love, that blood.

When he left I found before his chair
a blood-soaked rag, from the bandage,
a rag fit for the trash heap at that instant;
and that I took to my lips,
and that I held close a long time—
love's blood resting on my lips.

Coins

Coins with Indian inscriptions.
Referring to monarchs of the greatest power,
to Eboukratintaza, to Strataga,
to Menantraza, to Eramaiaza.
So the learned book renders for us
the Indian writing on one side of the coins.
But the book shows us the other side as well,
which is, moreover, the good side
with the figure of the king. And how instantly he stops here,
how deeply moved he is, the Greek who reads in Greek
Hermaios, Ephkratides, Straton, Menander.

Taken

These days I've been reading folk songs,
the exploits and the wars of mountain rebels,
agreeable matters; ours, Greek matters.

I've also read the laments for Constantinople's fall:
"They've taken the City, they've taken her; they've taken Saloniki."
And while the two were chanting,
"on the left the king, on the right the patriarch,"
a Voice was heard and it told them to be silent now,
"priests, stop your psalms and close the gospels;"
they've taken the City, they've taken her; they've taken Saloniki.

Yet more than all the rest the song of Trebizond
moved me, with its peculiar language
and with the sorrow of those distant Greeks
who maybe through it all believed that we would still be saved.

But alas a fateful bird "comes from the City"
bearing in its "wing a paper black with writing
not lighting in the vineyard, or even in the orchard
it went on till it came to earth where the cypress roots."
The archbishops can't (or do not wish) to read,
"It's Johnny, oh, the widow's boy," he takes the paper,
and he reads it and he keens.
"Him reading so, him weeping so, his heart a thunder sounding.
Here's doom to us, here's woe to us, Imperial Greece is taken."

From the Drawer

I'd intended to place it on a wall in my room.

But the dampness of the drawer has marred it.

I won't put this photograph in a frame.

I should have taken better care of it.

Those lips, that face—
oh that for just a day, for one hour
only, their past might come again.

I won't put this photograph in a frame.

I'll bear with seeing it marred this way.

Besides, even if it were not marred,
it would irk me to be on my guard lest
some word, some tone of voice betray me—
if they ever questioned me about it.

The Regiment of Pleasure

Do not speak of guilt, do not speak of responsibility. When the Regiment of Pleasure passes with music and flags; when the senses shudder and tremble, whoever stays far off is foolish and impious, whoever does not rush to the beautiful campaign, the going forth to conquest of felt joys and of passions.

All morality's laws—badly thought out, badly applied—are worth nothing and not able to stand for even a moment, when the Regiment of Pleasure passes with music and flags.

Do not allow any shady virtue to restrain you. Do not believe that any obligation binds you. Your obligation is to yield, to yield always to Desires, which are the most perfect creations of the perfect gods. Your obligation is to enlist as faithful soldier, with perfect simplicity of heart, when the Regiment of Pleasure passes with music and flags.

Do not shut yourself in your house and cleverly fool yourself with theories of justice, with society's badly made superstitions about recompense. Do not say, My effort is worth so much, and so far may I take hold of joy. Just as life is an inheritance which you did nothing to earn as a reward, so must Pleasure also not be a reward. Do not shut yourself in your house; but keep the windows open, fully open, so you may hear the first sounds of the soldiers' marching, when the Regiment of Pleasure arrives with music and flags.

Do not be deceived by however many blasphemers may tell you the service is dangerous and hard. The service of pleasure is permanent joy. It exhausts you, but it exhausts you with divine frenzy. And at last when you fall on the road, even then your lot is enviable. When your funeral goes in procession, the Forms who gave shape to your desires will cast cockscombs and bright roses on your coffin, the ephebic Gods of Olympus will raise you up on their shoulders, and they will bury you in the cemetery of the Ideal where the mausoleums of poetry glow white.

The Ships

From the Fantasy all the way to the Page. It is a difficult passage, it is a dangerous sea. The distance appears small at first sight, and all the same how long a journey it is, and how harmful sometimes for ships which attempt it.

The first danger springs from the extremely delicate nature of the goods which the ships convey. In the marketplaces of Fantasy, the majority and the best of things are constructed of fragile kinds of glass and diaphanous ceramics, and many break when they are unloaded on dry land. All of this damage is irreparable, because it is out of the question for the boat to turn back and retrieve similarly beautiful things. There is no possibility of the same shop that sold them being found. The marketplaces of Fantasy have grand and luxurious establishments, but no extended duration. Their commercial dealings are brief, they trade their goods swiftly, and liquidate immediately. It is very rare for a returning ship to find those same exporters with those same goods.

Another danger springs from the ships' provisions. They set out from the harbors of the opulent mainlands overloaded, and later when they find themselves on the open sea they are compelled to cast off some part of the load to save everything else. Consequently, practically no ship succeeds in bringing in intact as much treasure as it received. The things cast off are obviously the goods of least value, but it sometimes happens that the sailors, in their great hurry, will make mistakes and will cast into the sea objects of great value.

If, on the other hand, it arrives at the bright paper harbor, sacrifices will again be newly required. The customs officers come and examine one sort of cargo and consider whether they should permit its unloading; they refuse to allow any other goods to be unloaded; and of the one sort they in fact admit only a small quantity. The place has its laws. All commercial goods do not have free entry, and smuggling is strictly forbidden. The importing of wine is prohibited, because the mainlands from which the ships come make wines and spirits from grapes which a more clement temperature develops and ripens. The customs officials want none of those liquors. They are much too intoxicating. They are not suitable for all brains. Moreover, there exists a company in the place, which has a monopoly on wines. The color of that wine and the taste of that water have a thin body, and you can drink of these all day without getting at all dizzy. It is an old company. It enjoys great esteem, and its shares are always rising in value.

But, on the other hand, let us be satisfied when the ships enter the harbor, even if that involves all those sacrifices. Because in the end, through sleeplessness and much care, the number of shattered or cast-off pieces has been reduced during the length of the voyage. Additionally, the laws of the place and the regulated customs officers are, on the one hand tyrannical about many things, but not entirely deterrent, and the greater part of the cargo is unloaded. On the other hand, the officers of the customs house are not infallible, and a variety of the prohibited goods gets through inside falsely labeled crates that have one thing written on them and something else inside them, and some good wines are imported for the choice drinking parties.

Grievous, one other thing is grievous. It is when certain huge ships pass, with coral jewels and masts of ebony, with great flags unfurled white and red, filled with treasures, and none even come near the harbor, either because all the goods that they bring are prohibited, or because the harbor isn't deep enough to receive them. And they continue on their way. A favorable wind blows in their silken sails, the sun glazes the gleam of their golden bows, and they grow ever distant calmly and majestically, they grow always and forever more distant from us and from our narrow harbor.

Fortunately those ships are very rare. We scarcely see two or three throughout all our lives, and we forget them quickly. However bright the sight of them was, so rapid is their oblivion. And after a few years pass, if one day—while we are sitting sluggish looking at the light or listening to the silence—by chance the sound of those enthusiastic stanzas comes back into our minds, we don't remember them at first, and we torment our memory in order to recall where we heard them before. After much effort the old memory awakes and we recall that those stanzas are from the songs which the sailors sang, beautiful as the heroes of *The Iliad*, when the grand, the divine ships passed by and continued forward on their way—who knew where.

Garments

In a large box or in a bureau of highly valued ebony I will place and I will keep safe the garments of my life.

The blue clothes. And then the red, the most beautiful of all. And afterwards the yellow. And last again the blue, but these second much more faded than the first.

I will keep them safe with reverence and with much sorrow.

When I shall wear black clothes, and shall live in a black house, in one dark room, I shall at some time open the bureau with joy, with passion, and with despair.

I shall see the clothes and I will remember the great festival—which then will be in all ways ended.

In all ways ended. The furniture dispersed disorderly in the hallways. Plates and glasses broken on the ground. All the candles burned to the bottom. All the wine drunk. All the guests departed. A few tired ones will be sitting all alone, as I will be, in darkened houses—others more weary will have gone to sleep.

REJECTED POEMS: 1886–1898

Bacchic

Weary of the world's guileful inconstancy,
in my glass I have found peace;
life and hope therein and desires I enclose;
       give me to drink.

I feel distant here from life's disasters, its storms,
like a sailor who's been rescued from a shipwreck
and finds himself on a safe boat in a harbor.
       Give me to drink.

Oh, warmth of my wine, healthy, you keep away
everything cold that would flow in. Envy or disgrace,
or hate, or petty denigration, its chill does not touch me;
       give me to drink.

Graceless naked truth I see no longer.
I have enjoyed another life, I have a world that's new;
I find myself on the wide field of dreams—
       give, give me to drink!

And if it is a poison, and if I find the bitterness
of what ends all in it, I still have found happiness,
delight, joy, and sublime heights in the poison;
       give me to drink!

The Poet and the Muse

THE POET

What good, what profit did fortune seek,
that in my weakness I was made a poet?
My words are vain; my harp's sounds,
the most musical of them, are not true.

The noble feelings I may wish to hymn,
glory and virtue, I feel they're dreams.
Wherever I gaze, in every place I find discouragement,
and everywhere my foot gives way to thorns.

The earth's a dark sphere, cold and wily.
My songs are a deluding picture of the world.
Joy I sing, and the body's love. Vile parody,
vile harp, prey for every fraud!

THE MUSE

You are no liar, poet. The world that you
see is the true one. The harp's chords
alone know truth, and in this life
our certain guides are those alone.

You are the celebrant of divinity. It gave you
beauty's portion and spring's. Mellifluous song
flows from your lips, you are a treasury
of balm—golden promise and a voice from on high.

If the earth is hidden in darkness, do not fear.
Neither think the dark endures forever.
Friend, you are beside pleasures, flowers, valleys;
look to them, and fare forward. Behold what light begins!

Only a frail mist disturbs your gaze.
Beneath the veil gracious nature for you
prepares crowns of roses, and violets and noble
narcissi, your songs' fragrant recompense.

Builders

The act of building Progress is immense—everyone
brings his stone; one words, one counsel, another one
deeds—and daily it raises its head
higher. If a hurricane, some sea-swell

suddenly should come, the good workers throng
in one surge and defend the unavailing task.
Unavailing, because each one's life is spent
for future generations, suffering abuse, pain

for that generation to know authentic
happiness, and long life, and riches, and wisdom
without vile sweat, or servile work.

But this fictive generation will not ever live;
its own perfecting will be what destroys this building
and then those men's vain efforts will all begin anew.

Word and Silence

Iza kan elkalam min fidda, assoukout min zachab.
 —Arabic proverb

"Silence is golden and the word silver."

What profane character uttered such blasphemy?
What languishing Asian blind, mute, abandoned to blind,
mute fate? What madman, wretched,
stranger to mankind, reviling virtue,
said the soul is a chimera, and the word silver?
Our only gift suiting us to God, containing
all else—enthusiasm, sorrow, joy, love;
the sole thing human in our bestial nature!
    You who call it silver, you do not believe
in the future, dissolution of silence, mysterious word.
You do not grow tender in wisdom, progress does not charm you;
with ignorance—silver silence—you are gratified.
You are ill. Unfeeling silence is a grave malady,
while the Word, warm, empathic, is health.
Silence is shadow and night; the Word is day.
The Word is truth, life, immortality.
    We are to speak, we are to speak—silence does not suit us
since we were fashioned in the image of the Word.
We are to speak, we are to speak—since in us
divine thought speaks, the soul's unbodied speech.

Sam el Nesim

      Our pallid Egypt
      the sun burns, beats arrows into
with bitterness and with thirst
and with disease exhausts.
      Our sweet Egypt
      in a laughing festival
goes drunk, forgets, and adorns itself, and rejoices,
and affronts the tyrannical sun.

*

Joyous Sam el Nesim proclaims the spring,
      innocent festival of the country resorts.
Alexandria is emptied, and all her close-packed streets.
The good Egyptian wants to celebrate
joyous Sam el Nesim and goes off in a tent.
      From everywhere the thronging

battalions of holiday-lovers pour out. The Khambari fills
      and the pale blue, musing Mahmoudiya.
The Mex, Muharram Bey, the Ramleh are all filled.
And the rural spots compete over which will get
the most carts, on which the crowds of happy people arrive
      in solemn, peaceful mirth.

Because the Egyptian even in a festival
      preserves his solemn bearing.
He adorns his fez with blossoms; but his face
stays unexpressive. He murmurs a monotonous song,
happily. He enjoys things greatly in his thinking,
      minimally in his motions.

Our Egypt does not have abundant greenery,
      it has no pleasant streams or fountains,

it has no high mountains with broad shade.
But it has magic flowers, fallen flaming from
the torch of Ptah, breath from unknown aromatic
     myrrh, in which nature faints.

At the center of a marveling circle the sweet minstrel
     of far-reaching fame is applauded warmly.
In his trembling voice the pains of
eros sigh; his song complains bitterly
against the flighty Fatima or the severe Emene,
     against most wily Zenab.

By the shading tents and chilled sherbet
     the burning and the dust are routed.
The hours pass like minutes, like steeds quick
over a smooth plain, with their bright manes
gladly spread over the festival,
     gilding the joyous Sam el Nesim.

              *

     Our pallid Egypt
      the sun burns, beats arrows into
with bitterness and with thirst
and with disease exhausts.
     Our sweet Egypt
      in a laughing festival
goes drunk, forgets, and adorns itself, and rejoices,
and affronts the tyrannical sun.

Singer

Far from the world, poetic magic intoxicates him;
        beautiful verses are, for him, the whole world.
For her singer Fantasy has built
        a sturdy immaterial house that fortune does not shake.

You will say: "Cold and futile life. It is folly
        to think life is a flute of delighting
sounds, and nothing else"; or "Stale lack of feeling
        plagues one never wracked by the pain

of life's struggle." But your judgment
        is an error and injustice. His Nature is divine.
Do not judge from your logical, blind sickness.

His house's walls are made of magic emerald—
        in them voices whisper; "Friend, be at peace.
Think and sing. Mystic apostle, be brave!"

Vulnerant Omnes, Ultima Necat

The Metropolis of Bruges, which long ago
some mighty Flemish Duke had built and lavishly endowed,
has a clock with silver portals
that has been telling time from many ages past.

The Clock said: "My life is cold
          and colorless, and cruel.
Every day on earth is the same for me.
Friday and Saturday, Sunday, Monday,
have nothing different in them. I live—without hoping.
The only entertainment, the only variety
in my fated, bitter monotony
          is the world's destruction.
When, in decay, I turn my slothful fingers
all earthly fraudulence appears before me.
Ending and collapse everywhere. Loud sounds of struggles
never to be overcome, groans buzzing around me—and I conclude
     that
Each of my hours wounds; the last one murders."

The Archbishop heard the audacious speech
and said: "Clock, that language violates
the decorum of your ecclesiastical and exalted rank.
How did such a cunning thought
come into your mind? Oh foolish, heretical idea!
          It must be that boredom
has set a dense mist around your soul.
          The chorus of hours
received another mission from the Lord.
Each one again rekindles; the last gives birth."

Good and Bad Weather

It does not bother me if outside
winter spreads mists, clouds, and cold.
Within me spring goes on, true joy.
Laughter is a ray, all golden,
there is no other garden like love,
the warmth of song melts all snows.

What good is it that outside
spring brings flowers up and sows greenery!
Within me I have winter where the heart's in pain.
A sigh obscures the brightest sun,
when you have sorrow May is like December,
tears are colder than cold snow.

Timolaos the Syracusan

Timolaos is the first musician
in the first city of Sicily.
The Greeks of our Western Greece,
from Neapolis and Marseilles,
from Tarentum, Reggio, and Agrigento,
and from as many other cities on the shores
of Hesperia that they crown with Hellenism,
hurry in great numbers to Syracuse,
to hear the glorious musician.
Wisest with the lyre and the cithara,
he also knows the delicate pipe,
tenderest of all tender flutes. He draws forth
from the reed a weeping melody.
And when he takes his harp in hand,
its chords give out the poetry
of fervent Asia—initiation
to voluptuous and to sweet musing,
fragrances of Ecbatana and Nineveh.
. . . .
. . . .
But amid the many commendations,
amid gifts worth many talents,
the good Timolaos is all sorrow.
Free-flowing Samos wine does not delight him,
and silent he affronts the drinking party.
Some vague sorrow possesses him,
the sorrow of his great weakness.
He feels his organs empty,
while his soul's replete with music.
In vain he struggles, fixedly, with pain,
to pour out the climax of his secret notes;
his most accomplished harmonies stay

mute, made latent secrets in him.
The enthusiastic crowd marvels
at things he censures and disdains.
The voice of clamorous praises troubles him,
and amid gifts worth many talents
the musician stands abstractedly apart.

Athena's Vote

When no resolution in justice can be attained,
when the judgment of men is perplexed
and requires help and light from above,
the judges go silent, queasy, small,
and the compassion of the Gods decides things.

Pallas spoke to the citizens of Athens:
"I established your court. Not Greece,
not any other city could want to acquire
a more glorious one. Brave judges,
show yourselves worthy of it. Renounce
unbecoming passions. Have clemency
accompany justice. If your judgment
is austere, let it be clean
as well—immaculate as a diamond, pure.
Your work should show the way
for good and noble deeds, and moderate
command. Never follies of vengeance."

The men of the city answered, moved;
"O Lady, our thought is all unable
to find a tribute in gratitude sufficient
to the shining benefit you have conferred."

                    The grey-eyed
goddess answered them: "Mortals,
Divinity requires from you no wages.
Be virtuous and impartial;
this suffices me. In any case, brave judges,
I have the privilege of a single vote reserved."

The judges said: "Living
in the starry firmament, Goddess,
how do you cast your vote here with us?"

"Do not let
this question weary you. I am restrained
in the use of my vote. But if a moment comes
when you are divided into two factions,
one for, the other against, without my leaving
the rooms of heaven you will use
this vote of mine yourselves. Men of the city,
I wish you always to show mercy
to the accused. In the fervent soul
of your Athena dwells forgiveness,
vast, limitless,
and instinctive from Metis,
the crown of wisdom exalted in heaven."

The Inkwell

Sacred to the poet, honor-worthy inkwell,
    from whose interior a world goes forth,
each form, passing near to you,
    comes back with a newly special grace.
Where did your ink discover all this legendary
wealth! Its every drop, as it falls to the paper,
    sets another diamond down for us
    among the diamonds of fantasy.

Who taught you the words which, centered,
    you cast into the world, which bring enthusiasm to us;
and which the children of our children shall read
    with the same emotion and zeal.

Where did you find those words that in our ears,
    while they echo as things heard before,
still do not seem utterly unknown—
    in another life our heart surely knew them.

The pen you wet resembles a hand
    that turns on the clock of the soul.
The moments of feeling it counts and governs,
    the hours of the soul it counts and changes.

Sacred to the poet, honor-worthy inkwell,
    from whose ink a world goes forth—
the thought comes to me now how many people will stay
    lost inside you, when the deepest sleep
one night takes away the poet.
The words will be there always; but what unknown hand
    will be able to find them, to bring them to us!
    You, faithful to the poet, will deny them.

Sweet Voices

Those voices are sweetest which have forever
        gone still, which in
the sad heart alone resound mournfully.

In dreams they come fearful and humble,
        the melancholy voices,
and make us weak with the memory

of so many dead who were loved, whom cold
        the cold earth covers, for whom dawn
smiling never shines, and flowers do not open.

The melodious voices sigh; and in the soul
        the first poetry of our life
echoes—like music, nighttime's, distant.

Elegy of the Flowers

As many flowers as can be blossom in the summer.
    And of all the field's flowers youth
    looks most beautiful. But it withers
    quickly, and when it goes it has no second birth;
the jasmines sprinkle it with tears of dew.

As many flowers as can be blossom in the summer.
    But the same eyes do not look at them.
    And other hands place them on other breasts.
    The same months come, but they seem strangers;
the faces have changed and they're not recognized.

As many flowers as can be blossom in the summer.
    But they do not always stay while our joy does.
    Those which delight, those same ones embitter;
    and over graves, where we weep, they come forth
even as they color our laughing fields.

Again the summer's come and all the fields blossom.
    But getting there from the window's difficult.
    And the pane goes smaller-smaller, vanishes.
    The pained eye goes dull, is afflicted.
The weary feet, heavy, do not bear us up.

It's not for us that the fields bloom this year.
    Lilies of a forgotten August wreath our brows,
    our former years come rushing back,
    beloved shadows sweetly signal us
and sweetly cast a sleep over our poor heart.

Melancholy Hours

The fortunate desecrate Nature.
Earth is sorrow's shrine.
Dawn lets fall a tear of unknown pain;
the pale orphaned evenings mourn;
and the elected soul chants in deep distress.

I hear sighs in the breezes.
I see grievance on the lily.
I sense the rose's painful life;
the fields teem with mysterious sorrow;
and in the dense forest a sob resounds.

People honor the fortunate.
And false poets hymn them.
The pillars, though, of Nature are closed
to all those unconcerned and cruel who laugh,
strangers who laugh in a hapless land.

Oedipus

Written after reading a description of the painting
Oedipus and the Sphinx by Gustave Moreau

The Sphinx has fallen upon him
with teeth and nails outstretched
and with the full ferocity of life.
Oedipus fell at her first onslaught,
her first appearance horrified him—
until then he had never imagined
such a face or such talk.
But for all the monster's leaning
her two legs on Oedipus's breast,
he recovers quickly—and now
he has no fear of her at all, because he has
the solution ready and will win.
And yet he is not joyful over this victory.
His fully melancholy gaze
is not turned on the Sphinx, beyond
he sees the narrow road that leads to Thebes,
and that finally will end at Colonus.
And his soul is clearly and prophetically aware
that there the Sphinx will speak to him again with more
difficult and with more extensive
riddles that have no answer.

Ode and Elegy of the Roads

The walking of the first wayfarer;
the lively call of the first peddler;
the opening of the first window,
the first door—are the odes
the roads have in the morning.

The steps of the final wayfarer;
the peddler's final call;
the shutting of the doors and windows—
are the elegiac songs
the roads have in the evening.

By an Open Window

In the nighttime of fair autumn weather,
by an open window,
for whole hours, in perfect,
voluptuous quiet, I sit.
The leaves' light rain drops down.

The sigh of the perishable world
resounds in my perishable nature,
but it is a sweet sigh, it rises like a prayer.
My window opens an unknown
world. A fountain's offered me
of memories, fine-scented, inexpressible.
Over my window a wing
beats—fresh autumn spirits
come and circle round
and in their pure language speak to me.

I sense vague and extensive
hopes; and in the revered silence
of creation, my ears hear melodies,
hear crystalline, mystic
music from the chorus of the stars.

A Love

Disaster does not abate however much you speak of it.
But there are pains that in the heart do not keep still.
In complaint they thirst for release, for relief.

Antony loved me and I loved him.
And he gave me his word he would not take another!
But he was very poor and he had pride.
That is why he went away on a luckless ship
aiming to find work, to get a trade.
He wanted to become a sailor, and one day a captain,
and then to be married with his heart at peace.

Ah, a year was not yet done; and father falls
and breaks his leg and his right arm.
My mother got sick. Oh, what was left for us,
scant copper that was old, a little silver,
some small diamonds that mother had held on to,
were sold off for nothing.
                              Our disaster became
village gossip. The news was given out
from the grand houses, and from his manor
Stavros often came as friend and protector
to our house . . . and looked at me with love in his eyes.

My father didn't work. My mother did no embroidery.
Day and night I worked and poured out my eyesight
and despite it all I couldn't earn their bread.
Stavros was rich, with a big heart.
Simply—without boasting, without vain proclamations—
and secretly, he gave them means and kept them alive.
And my soul rejoiced for my poor parents—
and my soul wept for my poor self.
The unlucky day was not long delayed
on which in the field he stood beside me, and took

my hand and looked at me . . . I trembled like a leaf
because I knew what he wanted, and did not love him . . .
The words halted on his lips—until he said;
"Froso, will you not, for their sakes, consent to have me?"

No, my heart cried out to me seeking Antony.
But Boreas rose wild and heavy,
and people had said his boat was lost in foreign seas.
Ah, how did the cruel poisoned lie come out! . . .
Ah, how am I, a wretch, to live, to cry through night and day! . . .

My father said much to persuade me.
But my good mother said not a word to me,
she just looked me in the eye, and sorrow and poverty
ran down from her. I lost all strength.
I didn't bear up. I gave him my hand. Deep
my heart was buried, in the sea.

All the maidens of the village envied my luck
at getting a rich grandee for a husband,
village girl that I was, poor girl that I was.

Our village never saw a grander wedding
than ours. Young and old gathered to see
the lucky bride of the grandee.
They covered the road for us with lilacs and with roses.
Dances and music everywhere, songs and banquets.
It was night to me. All was dressed in black.

Four months only had passed since I'd taken him,
and one night, there where I stood all alone in the doorway
of my house, before me I see the ghost of Antony.
It seemed a dream to me, I did not believe my eyes;
until he said to me, "My love, why are you sad?
Our suffering is ended, I've come to make you mine."

Bitterly, bitterly I received him and told him everything.
And I clasped his hands as before in mine,
and I kissed him as before, and wept upon his neck.
I said that I loved no other but him...
I told him they'd misled me, how I believed
he'd drowned in a storm...How only for the sake
of my mother, my father I had married...How, together
with him, I preferred trials, poverty, and disdain
to all the wealth the earth has for another to bring...
I told him that I loved him as before, only now
my body's love is an unquenchable fire that burns me,
now that I know that never, never, never will he
become mine and I his...And I told him,
by his old love if a little of it remained,
to swear never to see me ever again in his life...
And I said other, other things; others I don't remember.
My head burned. I was losing my mind.

Now all those things have ended forever. My life's gone black.
This world never will hold joy for me.
Death should have laid hold of me!...But how am I to die—
I have a wound in my heart, but I am still young.

Memory

The gods do not die. The faith
    of the ungrateful mortal mob dies.
The gods are immortal. From our gazes
    silver clouds keep them hidden.
Oh sacred Thessaly, they love You still,
    their souls remember You.
In the gods, as in us, recollections flower,
    fervors of their first love.
When, erotic, the opening light of dawn kisses Thessaly,
    the early ecstasy of the gods' lives
passes through its atmosphere; and at times
    an ethereal figure flies up from its hills.

The Death of the Emperor Tacitus

The emperor Tacitus is ill.
His old age cannot bear up under,
cannot stand against the weight of toils in war.
In a loathsome camp confined to bed,
in vile Tyana—so far away!—

he remembers his beloved Campania,
his garden, his villa, his morning
walk—his life six months ago.—
And he curses in his agony
the Senate, the malicious Senate.

The Footsteps of the Eumenides

Nero sleeps in his royal palace
peacefully, unwitting and happy—
in the flesh's highest force,
in the beautiful crest of youth.

But his Lares are troubled.
The little gods of the hearth tremble,
and seek to hide their insignificant
bodies, to grow small, to vanish.
Because they've heard an inauspicious noise—
a noise of Tartarus, a noise of death—
coming from the staircase, and immediately
the cowardly Lares, with all their
sickened divinity fainting,
drew together, sensed, recognized
the fearful Eumenides' footsteps.

The Tears of the Sisters of Phaeton

Like light in matter, like diaphanous
gold is amber, precious amber.—
When a horrid manic power,
envying Phaeton, from the crest

of heaven hurled him,
his sisters came all in black
to his watery grave, Eridanus,
and daytime, nighttime they wept, the mournful ones.

And together with them all mortals keened
over the vanity of exalted dreams.
Oh heartless fortune, oh hateful destiny,
Phaeton fell from the clouds!

Within our humble homes
let us live satisfied with little, base;
let us put longings out of our hearts,
let there be an end to every urge toward heaven.

The wretched ones wept constantly,
the sisters wept for Phaeton,
and in every fold of the Eridanus
their ashen faces were reflected.

Extremely moved, the earth
received the nymph's reverend tears
and treasured them. Once seven days
had gone, and dawn shone on the eighth,

their many lamentations yielded
to eternal effulgence
and in shining amber were transfigured.
Oh choice stone! O virtuous tears!

Brave keening, enviable keening,
full of love and shining full—
honorable sisters, with tears of light
you mourned for the earth's most beautiful young man.

Ancient Tragedy

Ancient tragedy, ancient tragedy
is as sacred and far-reaching as the universe's heart.
A demos gave birth to it, a Greek city,
but it soared up at once, and in the heavens
               set the stage.

In an Olympian theater, in an arena worthy of them,
Hippolytus, Ajax, Alcestis, and Klaitemnestra
tell us of life terrible and empty
and mercy's drop falls to the grievous earth
               divine.

The people of Athens saw tragedy
in its younger form and marveled.
Tragedy flourished in the sapphire
theater of heaven. There it had as audience
the immortals. And the gods, upon great
pure diamond seats, heard in ineffable
pleasure the beautiful verses of Sophocles,
the pulsations of Euripides, the exaltedness of Aeschylus,
and the Attic fantasies of refined and tactful Agathon.
Actors worthy of the exalted dramas
were the Muses, Hermes, and the wise Apollo,
the beloved Dionysus, Athena, and Hebe.
And the vaults of heaven were replete with poetry;
the monologues resound, blessed and grievous;
and the choruses, inexhaustible springs of harmony;
and the sharp-minded dialogues' laconic phrases.
All nature, reverent, goes still, that tempest's noise
might not disturb the divine celebration.
Motionless and reverent, air, and earth, and sea
guarded the great gods' tranquility.
And at certain times there came to them an echo from the heights,

a bodiless clutch of flowers, a few verses,
with "Bravo, bravo," blended trimeters from the gods.
And air said to earth, and ancient earth to sea;
"Be still, be still; let us hear. In the heavenly
theater they are giving a performance of Antigone."

Ancient tragedy, ancient tragedy
is as sacred and far-reaching as the universe's heart.
A demos gave birth to it, a Greek city,
but it soared up at once, and in the heavens
                set the stage.

In an Olympian theater, in an arena worthy of them,
Hippolytus, Ajax, Alcestis, and Klaitemnestra
tell us of life terrible and empty
and mercy's drop falls to the grievous earth
                divine.

Horace in Athens

In the hetaera Leah's room,
where there is refined grace, wealth, a soft bed,
a young man, with jasmine in his hands, speaks.
Many stones adorn his fingers,

and he wears a white himation of pure silk
with eastern needlework in red.
His language is Attic and pure,
yet a touch of accent in pronunciation

betrays the tones of Tiber and of Latium.
The young man tells his love,
and the Athenian woman hears in silence

her eloquent lover Horace;
and marveling she beholds new worlds of Beauty and the Good
within the passions of the great Italian.

The Tarantians Divert Themselves

Theaters crammed, everywhere music;
here debauchery and license, and there
athletic and sophistic contests.
A wreath that does not wither adorns the statue of
Dionysus. No corner of earth remains dry
of libations. The townsmen of Tarantios divert themselves.

But the senators draw apart from all that
and scowling utter angry things.
And each barbarian toga on its way
seems a cloud cruelly promising a storm.

The Funeral of Sarpedon

The heart of Zeus is filled with grief.
Patroklos has killed Sarpedon.

The God respects Fate's will.
But the father mourns his misfortune.

The unvanquished son of Menoitos,
the Achaians roaring like lions,
seek to seize the dead man, and throw
him to the crows and dogs as food.

But Zeus does not consent to that disgrace.
He will not allow them to abuse
the body of his beloved and honored son.

See how from his chariot, by order,
Phoibos comes to earth.
His godly hands preserve
the dead Sarpedon, and he takes him
to the river and reverently washes him.
He cleanses the dust and thick blood,
and restores the bodily form
of the righteous and brave hero.
Phoibos lavishly pours the scents
of ambrosia upon the corpse,
and he dresses him with Olympian,
immortal clothes. His breast's
gaping wound he closes. He gives
the limbs a peaceful, graceful posture.
He whitens his skin. With rays of light
he combs his hair, abundant and
black hair, long and carefully
he makes the hair gleam.

                        He seems
a young athlete at rest—like a young lover
dreaming of happiness and love
with blue wings and a rainbow—
like a young and prosperous husband,
lucky in all his affairs,
having won a good wife and sponsors.

His command completed, the God
calls the brothers Sleep and Death,
and orders that Sarpedon be carried
to extensive Lykia.

As in fatherly and tender embrace
Sleep and Death received him,
with sorrow and with love and with care,
lest the dead face's sober calm
be disturbed, lest the ceremony
wound the heroic body.

The Lykians deeply reverenced
the fearful heartlessness of the Gods,
and bore to the king's palace
the dead spirit, in the nonetheless shining form,
strong, fragrant, and calm.

They found him a marble tomb,
and at its base in skilled carving
in relief they told the story of his
heroic victories and his many campaigns.

Voice from the Sea

The sea lets forth a secret voice—
    a voice that comes
into our heart and moves it
    and gives it joy.

The sea chants to us a tender song,
a song that three great poets made,
    the sun, the air, and the sky.
She chants it with that godly voice of hers,
when summer weather spreads calm
    upon her shoulders like a dress for her to wear.

Her melody carries dewy memories
to souls. Youth that's past
    she brings to mind without bitterness and without sorrow.
Past loves speak secretly,
forgotten feelings live again
    within the sweet breathing of the waves.

The sea chants to us a tender song,
a song that three great poets made,
    the sun, the air, and the sky.
And as you look at her watery plain,
as you see the green in her unbounded,
    her field that is close and so far off,

filled with yellow flowers that the sun
seeds like a gardener, joy takes you
    and intoxicates you, and it elevates your heart.
And if you are young, in your veins will run
the yearning of the sea; the wave will say one
word to you from its erotic life, and it will water
    your erotic life with mystical fragrance.

The sea lets forth a secret voice—
    a voice that comes
into our heart and moves it
    and gives it joy.

Is it a song, or a grievance of the drowned?—
The tragic grievance of the dead,
    who have the cold foam as their shroud,
and who weep for their wives, for their children,
and their parents, for their deserted nest,
    while the bitter sea tosses them about,

onto rocks and sharp stones it thrusts them,
it braids them among the sea's weeds, it drags, it ousts them,
    and they run as though alive
with their eyes all fright, throughout the night,
and with their hands wild, outstretched,
    from their agony, that last one.

Is it a song, or a grievance of the drowned?—
The tragic grievance of the dead
    who yearn for a Christian cemetery.
A grave, which relatives sprinkle with tears,
and decorate from loving hands with flowers,
    and where the sun pours out in a rush warm and
        compassionate light.

A grave that the all-immaculate Cross guards,
where at times some priest will go
    to burn incense and to say a prayer.
A widow brings him, that remembers her husband
or son, or sometimes a friend in sorrow.
They commemorate the one who has died; and the soul
    then sleeps in greater peace, forgiven.

319

Notes on Selected Poems

POEMS: 1905–1915

THE SATRAPY

Satrapies were administrative territories governed by satraps, officials of the Persian monarchy. Artaxerxes became king of Persia after the death of his father, Xerxes, in 464 B.C.E. Susa, "city of lilies," capital of the Achaemenid Persian dynasty, was the site of a palace and monumental gateway built by Darius I (521–486 B.C.E.), grandfather of Artaxerxes.

THE GOD FORSAKES ANTONY

Dionysus, deity of ecstatic sensual abandon, Antony's patron, is the departing god alluded to in the title. See Plutarch's *Life of Antony*, and Shakespeare's *Antony and Cleopatra*, act 4, scene 3.

THEODOTOS

According to Plutarch's *Life of Pompey*, Theodotos was a Greek from Chios who earned his living teaching rhetoric. A preeminent rival of Julius Caesar, Pompey the Great, born in 106 B.C.E., was assassinated and decapitated in Alexandria on September 28, 48 B.C.E., the day after his fifty-eighth birthday. Theodotos carried the head to Caesar, who was reported to have turned away in horror and wept at the sight.

KING DIMITRIOS

Dimitrios I of Macedonia, "Besieger of Cities" (336–283 B.C.E.), was proclaimed king of Macedonia in 295 after murdering Alexander V. In 288, during an expansive imperial maneuver, his armies deserted him to form an alliance with Pyrrhus, king of Epiros. He is famous for the mystification of regal authority, which Cavafy shows him shunning in this poem. See Plutarch's *Life of Dimitrios*.

THE GLORY OF THE PTOLEMIES

The title refers to the Macedonian dynasty that ruled Egypt after Alexander named all its kings Ptolemy. The king here, Lagides, is Ptolemy I Sotir ("Savior") (367/6–282 B.C.E.), son of Lagus (a lowborn Macedonian from whom the dynasty takes its familial name) and Arsinoe, childhood friend of Alexander and later one of his generals and author of a history of the conqueror's reign. The Selefkos named here (358–281 B.C.E.), (commonly spelled Seleucus, although I've kept the Greek lettering throughout the appearance of the Seleucids in these poems), was the first ruler of the Seleucid dynasty, which stretched from Turkey to central Asia in the Hellenistic period. The city referred to is Alexandria.

THE BATTLE OF MAGNESIA

Philip V (238–179 B.C.E.) was the last Macedonian king of that name. He carried out a series of failed military attempts to extend Macedonian influence west from Macedonia, fighting the Romans on the eastern shore of the Adriatic, and east, battling the Seleucid empire of Antiochus III, the Great (242–187 B.C.E.). Philip's final defeat, at the hands of the Romans, came at Cynoscephalae, in Thessaly, in 197 B.C.E., after which he was confined, under humiliating terms, to Macedonia. Antiochus, a sometime ally of Macedonia's against Rome, withheld his aid from Philip in that battle. Seven years later, in January 189 B.C.E., Antiochus was defeated by Rome's L. Cornelius Scipio Asiagenes at Magnesia, a city in Ionia. The Romans regarded Philip as a somewhat decadent Oriental potentate.

THE DISPLEASURE OF SELEFKIDES

Dimitrios Selefkides (187–150 B.C.E.) was the second son of Seleucus IV (218–174 B.C.E.). In keeping with the continual political skirmishing of the Roman and Seleucian empires, Rome held Dimitrios hostage for sixteen years, until 162 B.C.E. The Ptolemy who's come to Rome in this poem is Ptolemy VI, Philometor ("Mother-loving") (180–145 B.C.E.). Philometor reigned jointly with his sister/wife, Cleopatra II, and son Ptolemy VII, Neos Philopator ("Young, Father-loving"), and Ptolemy VIII, Euergetes II ("Benefactor"), from 169 to 164 B.C.E. In 164 B.C.E. his brother Ptolemy VIII exiled him from Alexandria and the throne. That year he traveled to Rome to seek restoration of his kingship. The Odyssean tale of Ptolemy VI's adopting shabby dwelling and demeanor to supplicate the Roman powers is told in Polybius's *Histories*. Polybius (200–118 B.C.E.) was a Greek historian who chronicled the cultural and political history of Rome's ascending dominion over the Mediterranean. He insisted that history was explanation that concentrated on the polyvalent reasons, by which he meant decisions, leading to the beginning, or the undertaking, of actions.

OROPHERNIS

Cappadocia is a region in east central Turkey. From 300 to 200 B.C.E., ruled variously and intermittently by the Ariarthan familial dynasty, whose members were regularly ousted by philhellenic Roman and Syrian kings, Asiatic Cappadocia took on a Greek cultural gleam in its language, institutions, and modes of life. Ionia is a region on the central coast of Asia Minor that includes a number of the Aegean Islands. The ancient Ionians had claimed descent from the Athenians, a claim the Hellenistic Ionians maintained. Orophernis was the son of Ariarthis IV, Eusebes ("Reverent") (220–163 B.C.E.), a Hellenistic Iranian king of Cappadocia. During Orophernis's life the Cappadocian court was famous for its Hellenistic cultivation, especially during the reign of his brother Ariarthis V, Eusebes Philopator ("Reverent, Father-loving") (163–130 B.C.E.). The Dimitrios mentioned here is Dimitrios Sotir ("Savior") of Syria (187–150 B.C.E.), primary mover of the Syrian force that made Orophernis king briefly in 157 B.C.E., until he was ousted by his brother Ariarthis V. (See the notes for "The Displeasure of Selefkides" and "Of Dimitrios Sotir [162–150 B.C.].") Orophernis failed in the later attempt, narrated here, to take Sotir's throne, and died in 154 B.C.E.

ALEXANDRIAN KINGS

In 34 B.C.E., to celebrate Mark Antony's annexation of Armenia, Cleopatra VII (69–30), the protagonist of plays by Shaw and Shakespeare, appeared in Alexandria as Isis in a magnificent ceremony arranged by Antony. His intention was to commemorate the divisions of Alexander the Great's Egyptian kingdom by symbolically parceling out that kingdom to Cleopatra, their two sons, and one son of Julius Caesar's. Alexander Helios ("Sun") was named king east of the Euphrates, his brother Ptolemy Philadelphus was named king west of the Euphrates, and Cleopatra was given the title Selene ("Moon") and made queen of Cyrene. Cleopatra and Kaisarion, her thirteen-year-old son, allegedly by Julius Caesar, ruled Egypt and Cyprus, respectively, as Queen of Kings and King of Kings. After the ceremony, which those hostile to Antony regarded as a parody of the Roman triumphal march of military victors to the temple of Jupiter on the Capitol, the mother and children took a progress through Alexandria dressed in the dynastic costumes of their titular realms.

PHILHELLENE

A fictional monarchical figurehead in Parthia, ruling over the Seleucid satrapy Phraata, now eastern Iran, orders currency minted for his realm. Zagros is a mountain conjoining the Median and Assyrian dominions.

THE FOOTSTEPS

Nero (37–68 C.E.) was emperor of Rome from 54 to 68 C.E. (See the note for "Nero's Term.") In 59, Nero had his mother, Iulia Agrippina, killed for her disapproval of his romance with Poppaea Sabina. His father was Domitius Aenobarbus. Lares are minor Roman deities who protect households in which proper homage is paid to ancestral spirits. The Erinyes, minor but effective Greek deities, punish familial wrongdoing, especially murder.

HERODIS ATTIKOS

Claudius Atticus Herodes (101–177 C.E.), friend and teacher of the Roman emperor and philosopher Marcus Aurelius (121–180), was a celebrated Sophist and architectural benefactor in Athens. Alexander the Selefkian was nicknamed the Clay Plato.

TYANAN SCULPTOR

Tyana was a city in Cappadocia. Rhea, Saturn's wife, was mother of the Olympian gods and daughter of Heaven and Earth. For Pompey, see the note for "Theodotos." Marius (157–86 B.C.E.), Aemilius Paulus (died 160 B.C.E.), and Scipio Africanus Major (236–183 B.C.E.) or Minor (185–129 B.C.E.) were all also heroic Romans, consuls, and generals. Kaisarion, Ptolemy XV, was born in 47 B.C.E., the eldest son of Cleopatra VII and, by her claim, Julius Caesar. He was executed by Caesar Augustus in 30 B.C.E. Hermes, son of Zeus and the nymph Maia, is the messenger of the gods, and, among his many other functions—guide of travelers, protector of children, patron of herdsmen—he escorted the dead to Hades. He is typically portrayed in sculpture carrying the caduceus, the herald's sign, wearing a traveler's hat that is sometimes winged, and shod with winged sandals to denote the speed and range of his travels.

THAT'S THE MAN

Antioch was the capital of Syria; Edessa the capital of Osroini, a kingdom in Mesopotamia. Lucian of Samosota (born c.120 C.E.) wrote in many literary forms, all of which he handled with comedy, which ranged from mean-spirited cynicism to sophisticated bemusement. As he portrays the event in his piece "Dream," the phrase "that's the man" was uttered by Culture to Lucian. Culture promises to make Lucian so conspicuously accomplished a writer that whenever he is in a foreign place people will see the marks of genius on him and whisper to one another, "That's the man."

DANGEROUS REMARKS

The two August rulers mentioned in this poem are sons of Constantine the Great (272–337 C.E.), who jointly ruled the eastern Roman Empire, seated in Constantinople, after their father's death. Konstantinos died in

340, after which his brother ruled until his assassination, at a soldier's hands, in 350.

MANUEL KOMNINOS
Manuel I Komninos ruled Byzantium as emperor from 1143 to 1180. The Orthodox Church increasingly disapproved of him as his reign went on, for his friendliness toward Rome, and especially for his indefatigable, profligate, and remorseless lechery. As he was dying, Manuel's court astrologers predicted he would live fourteen more years. He finally lost faith in them in mid-September of 1180, when he formally renounced them and shed his emperor's clothes for a monk's robe. He died September 24, 1180.

POEMS: 1916–1918

BEFORE THE STATUE OF ENDYMION
Endymion, a mythological shepherd, asked Zeus to grant him eternal youth and the power to sleep prodigiously. Selene, goddess of the moon, saw Endymion sleeping naked on Mount Latmos, near Miletos, in Asia Minor, and, enamored, made somnolent love to him nightly. Latmos was also held, by some, to be the grave of Endymion.

ENVOYS FROM ALEXANDRIA
The rival kings are Ptolemy VI, Philomotor, and his brother Ptolemy VIII, Euergetes II, who ruled Egypt jointly from 169 to 164 B.C.E. In 164, Philometor pled for his throne in Rome. In 163 he was restored as the Alexandrian monarch, and Euergetes II was given the kingdom of Cyrene to rule.

ARISTOVOULOS
The Asmonaean dynasty, a line of the Maccabees, ruled Judea from 142 to 63 B.C.E. Herod the Great (73–4 B.C.E.), declared king of Judea in 40, united warring branches of the Asmonaean dynasty by marrying Miriam in 37. Alexandra, the protagonist of this poem, was the mother of Miriam and Aristovoulos, and hence Herod's mother-in-law. Kypros was Herod's mother, and Salome his sister. Aristovoulos's far-famed beauty attracted the attention at one point of Cleopatra's consort, Mark Antony. The attention did him little good, since, in 35, Herod did the bidding of his

mother and sister and had the beautiful young man drowned in an all-too-typical consolidation of monarchical dominion.

KAISARION

Kaisarion was born in 47 B.C.E., the son of Cleopatra VII and, by rumor, Julius Caesar. Mark Antony installed him as coruler of Egypt with his mother in 34 B.C.E. The claimed descent from Caesar made Kaisarion a blood rival of Octavian, Caesar Augustus, who had Kaisarion executed after the seventeen-year-old king's tutor betrayed him to Rome's emperor, in 30 B.C.E. According to Plutarch's *Life of Antony*, Octavian ordered the execution after consulting Arrius, an Alexandrian philosopher, who advised the emperor as follows: "Too many *Caesars* are not well." Hence the phrase "too many Caesars," with which Cavafy closes the poem.

NERO'S TERM

Nero Claudius Caesar (37–68 C.E.) was emperor of Rome from 54 to 68. Nero was a Grecophile who transformed Rome's gladiatorial combat into Greek athletics and brought Greek arts, especially music and recitation, into high prominence in Rome. In 67, on an expedition to exuberantly experience Greek entertainments, Nero also visited the Delphic oracle. In 68, the Roman army requested of Galba, Spain's Roman governor, that he take up the imperial throne. Nero returned to Rome in 68, where the Senate declared him a public enemy. He committed suicide at the villa of his freedman Phaeon shortly after Galba, then seventy-three years old, accepted the army's promotion. At the end Nero declared, "What an artist dies with me!"

IN A TOWN OF OSROINI

Osroini is located in northwestern Mesopotamia. Charmides (died 403 B.C.E.) was a noble Athenian, uncle to Plato. He was famous for his beauty, and appears in the Platonic dialogue that bears his name. *The Charmides*, an inquiry into temperance set in a palaestra (a wrestling ground/gymnasium), begins, comically, with Socrates involved in an inflamed sexual competition for this paragon of male beauty.

IN THE MONTH OF ATHYR

Athyr, October 10 to November 8 in the Egyptian calendar, was also goddess of tombs and of sexual love. The Greek letters *kappa* and *zeta* are an alphabetical form for the number 27.

POEMS: 1897–1908 *excluded from* POEMS: 1905–1915 *and* POEMS: 1916–1918

THE FIRST STEP
Theocritus (310–245 B.C.E.), a renowned poet of Greece born in Syracuse, is most famous for drawing forth unprecedented beauty from the pastoral form.

INTERRUPTION
Demeter is the goddess of earthly fecundity; Thetis, a sea nymph, is the mother of Achilles. Demeter, while rendering the infant Demophon immortal in a fire ritual, was interrupted by his mother, Metaneira, queen of Eleusis, who plucked the child from the fire. Thetis, while similarly burning away Achilles' mortality, was interrupted by her mortal husband, Peleus, father of Achilles, and king of Phtia.

THERMOPYLAE
The story of the battle of Thermopylae is told in Herodotus's *History*, books 5, 7, and 9. Thermopylae, which takes its name from the hot baths in the region, is a small pass in Thessaly, between the mountains and the sea. It was the main route from northern to central and southern Greece in antiquity. In 480 B.C.E., Thermopylae was the site of a battle that started on August 7 and lasted for three days. During the battle six thousand to seven thousand Greeks, led by Leonidas of Sparta, fought to hold back the invading Persian army, one hundred thousand strong by legends, led by Xerxes. The small band of Spartans directly under Leonidas's command amounted to three hundred men. On the third day Ephialtis, a local Greek, revealed an alternative route to the battle site, through which a Medean division of the Persians approached to attack Thermopylae from the rear. The Greek army retreated when they learned that the route had been opened, due to the treachery of Ephialtis and the departure of the Phocian allies who had been guarding it. Leonidas and his three hundred Spartans stayed and, except for one soldier, were all slaughtered. The survivor was reviled upon returning to Sparta for preferring life to glorious death.

CHE FECE. . . . IL GRAN RIFIUTO
The title is from Dante's *Inferno*, Canto 3, line 60, *"che fece per viltade il gran rifiuto,"* "who made through cowardice the grand refusal." The sinners punished there, "those who lived without disgrace and without praise,"

chase in scattered circles after a banner that flutters wildly in a wind storm just inside the gates of Hell. The naked racers howl from the suffering induced by the horseflies and wasps that continually sting them. These souls refused to take action at moments of moral crisis, and they have been denied entrance to Hell proper, because there they would provide those damned for their moral choices some occasion for self-esteem. The particular refusing soul Dante singles out is most likely Pope Celestine V, who was elected in July 1294 and then abdicated five months later, making way for Boniface VIII, who reigned from 1294 to 1303. It was Boniface for whom Dante expresses his most unreserved contempt in the *Commedia*.

THE HORSES OF ACHILLES
Achilles' horses were named Xanthos and Balios. They were conceived by Zephyros, the West Wind, with Podarge, a minor storm goddess. Their origin is given in book 16 of *The Iliad*, lines 149 to 154; their grieving over Patroklos, and Zeus's ruing of his donation of them to Peleus, occur in book 17, lines 426 to 447.

THE FUNERAL OF SARPEDON
Zeus spares his son Sarpedon, a Trojan, from death as long as he can in Homer's *Iliad*, but he finally consents to the son's death at Patroklos's hand in book 15. Hera plans the rescue of Sarpedon's body and the bearing of it to Lykia by Sleep and Death in book 16, just before Patroklos kills him. In the same book Zeus sends Apollo (Phoibos) to rescue and restore Sarpedon's body, and have it borne by Sleep and Death back to Lykia.

UNPUBLISHED POEMS: 1919–1932

IMENOS
Michael the Third (839–867 C.E.) was emperor of Byzantium from 842–867. His epithet was "the Drunkard."

OF DIMITRIOS SOTIR (162–150 B.C.)
Dimitrios I of Syria (187–150 B.C.E.) was the second son of Seleucus IV. At the age of nine, he was sent to Rome, where he remained a hostage until he was twenty-five. Then he found his way back to Syria, where he regained the throne by assassinating his cousin Antiochus V, a deed for which he took the title Sotir, "Savior."

He was never able to save himself, however; his reign was wrecked by alienation of old political allies, melancholy, and drunkenness. For "the battle of Magnesia," see the note to the poem that bears that title. The Macedonian conquest referred to is Alexander's; the dynasties referred to include the Seleucid and the Ptolemaic. Herakleidis was a onetime satrap of Babylon. Alexander Valas schemed with him to gain the Syrian throne, and did so by killing Dimitrios in 150. The poem presents Dimitrios's stoical retrospective view of worldly rule, and signals that by placing the dates of his reign in the title. See also the note for "The Displeasure of Selefkides."

IF ACTUALLY DEAD
Apollonios of Tyana was a first-century Greek philosopher credited with thaumaturgic powers akin to Christ's. His story is told in *The Life of Apollonios of Tyana*, by Philostratos, a Greek historian who died approximately 249 C.E. Justin the Elder is Justin I, Byzantine emperor from 518 to 527, who effected a brief reconciliation between the eastern and western churches in 519.

YOUNG MEN OF SIDON (400 A.D.)
Sidon was a cosmopolitan, Hellenized port city of Phoenicia, present-day Lebanon. Meleager, whose career peaked in 100 B.C.E., was a philosopher and poet from Syria who lived in Tyre, a town often paired with Sidon in the narration of Christ's preaching in the New Testament. Krinagoras, who lived from the first century B.C.E. to approximately 11 C.E., was an epigrammatist from Mytiline, a city on the Aegean island of Lesbos, off the Turkish shore. He made three trips to Rome and wrote epigrams about Cleopatra and Tiberius, among others. Rhianos, a poet and scholar from Crete, was born in 275 B.C.E. He was an editor of Homer, and also wrote erotic epigrams and epic poetry, which survive only in scant fragments. Aeschylus, commonly regarded as the greatest of the Athenian tragedians, was born at Eleusis in 525/4 B.C.E. and died in Gela, in Sicily, in 456/5 B.C.E. Aeschylus fought in the battle of Marathon, in 490 B.C.E., in which the Greeks routed the invading Persians. The epigram referred to in stanza 3 was composed by Aeschylus for his grave; it is famous, or infamous, for omitting all reference to his literary career and for vaunting about his soldierly part in the Marathon victory against Datis and Artaphernis, Persian leaders defeated there. The titles cited in the last stanza are all plays by Aeschylus, except for *Kassandra*. Agamemnon's Trojan concubine, Kassandra is a character in the *Oresteia*; no extant classical tragedy is titled for her.

DAREIOS

The poem is set in Amisos, a city on the coast of the Black Sea that the Romans conquered in 71 B.C.E. Dareios I (521–486 B.C.E.) was king of Persia when the battle of Marathon occurred, in 490 B.C.E. Mithridates VI Evpator ("Good Father") was a Persian king of Pontos from 120 to 63 B.C.E.

ANNA KOMNINA

Anna Komnina (1083–1146 C.E.), daughter of Alexios I Komninos, emperor of Byzantium from 1081 to 1118, was one of the earliest women historians and a preeminent writer of the Byzantine world. The *Alexiad*, written in Anna's later years and finished by 1148, is more an encomium to her father than a history, and is notable for its characteristic Orthodox hostility to the Roman Church, especially to the first Crusade, which took place during her father's reign. At her father's death Anna conspired, with no success, to depose her younger brother John, named heir by their father, in favor of her husband, Nicepherous Bryennius. After her husband's death she withdrew to a convent, where she wrote the *Alexiad*. In the chapter narrating her emperor-father's death, Anna omits the bestowal of succession on her brother John, whom she refers to without naming him, unlike Cavafy in this poem.

A BYZANTINE GENTLEMAN, IN EXILE, COMPOSING VERSES

Nikiphoros III Botanaitis became emperor of Byzantium by ousting Michael VII, in 1078. In 1081, Botanaitis was ousted by Alexios I Komninos, whose wife, Irini Doukana, is referred to in this poem.

THE FAVOR OF ALEXANDER VALAS

Alexander Valas became king of Syria by ousting Dimitrios Sotir in 150 B.C.E. His reign was short; he died in 145 B.C.E.

MELANCHOLY OF JASON KLEANDER;
POET IN KOMMAGINI; 595 A.D.

Kommagini is located on the western bank of the Upper Euphrates. It passed historically from Assyrian to Seleucid to Persian to Byzantine to Arab rule. The period referred to in this poem is during Byzantine rule.

DIMARATOS

Porphyry (234–305 C.E.) was a scholar and philosopher who also wrote on the history of religion and literary form. In Rome Porphyry was the student of Plotinus (205–269/70 C.E.), the preeminent Neoplatonic philosopher, whose works Porphyry edited. *The Cave of the Nymphs*, Porphyry's allegorizing commentary on the Calypso episode in *The Odyssey*, is a famous example of classical allegorizing of moral personality in terms of the soul's choice of actions in the dangerous world of matter. The term *character* refers to a minor genre in Greek classical writing invented by Theophrastus (372/1–288/7 B.C.E.), who succeeded Aristotle after that philosopher withdrew from Athens and the academy at the death of Alexander in 323 B.C.E. Theophrastus's book *Characters* is made up of thirty short comic sketches describing types of failed personality, social more than moral: the complainer, the boaster, the flatterer, and so forth. The pairing of Porphyry and Theophrastus at the beginning of the poem suggests that Cavafy has in mind a seriocomic portrayal of Dimaratos's vindictiveness and quest for just retrieval of his Spartan throne. Dimaratos reigned as king of Sparta jointly with Kleomenis from 515 to 491 B.C.E. In 491, Kleomenis schemed with Leotychidis to have Dimaratos deposed through an announcement by the bribed Delphic oracle that Dimaratos was not the legitimate heir to the throne. Leotychidis took the throne, and Dimaratos sought refuge with Dareios, king of Persia. The Greeks, as Dimaratos had feared, did end up winning against the Persians in a sea battle off Cape Mycale, in 479 B.C.E. In that battle the Greeks were led by Leotychidis and the Persians by Xerxes. This poem presents Dimaratos, at the end of a twelve-year Persian exile, preparing Xerxes for that battle.

FROM THE SCHOOL OF THE RENOWNED PHILOSOPHER
Ammonius Sakkas (died 243 C.E.) was a Platonist philosopher who taught in Alexandria in the first half of the third century C.E. Born a Christian, he embraced pagan thought in his young manhood. His nickname, "Sack Carrier," or "Sackcloth Wearer," implies a humble origin, and that, together with his charismatic intimacy with his students, and the fact that he wrote nothing, earned him the title "Socrates of the Neoplatonists." His students included the great Neoplatonist Plotinus, the Greek Orthodox Church father Origen (185–255 C.E.), and the literary theoretician Longinus (first century C.E.).

CRAFTSMAN OF WINEBOWLS
Herakleidis was the treasurer of Antiochus IV Epiphanis (215–164 B.C.E.), who reigned as king of Persia from 175 to 165 B.C.E. The battle of Magnesia, in which Antiochus IV's father, Antiochus III, played a significant part by his absence, took place in 189 B.C.E., indicating that the poem refers to the year Antiochus IV ascended to the Persian throne.

THOSE WHO FOUGHT FOR THE ACHAIAN ALLIANCE

Achaia is a region in the northeast Peloponnese in Greece. The Achaian Alliance was a federal organization, entered into by the twelve cities of Achaia, that issued currency, conferred citizenship, and fought wars and made peace with Greek city-states and foreign states. The first alliance, in which relations were mostly between Athens, Sparta, and Macedonia, was established in 446 B.C.E. and dissolved in the last third of the fourth century B.C.E. It was revived in 280 B.C.E., and for almost 135 years, the Achaian Alliance carried out military conflicts in which Sparta and Macedonia were alternately its allies and enemies, depending on the resistance of any one of these powers toward Rome at any moment. Rome proved more powerful, and in the Achaian War, fought in 146/5 B.C.E., conquered Achaia and dissolved the alliance. Diaios and Kritolaos were the losing generals of the alliance in this conflict. Lathyros (a nickname meaning "Chickpea") was Ptolemy IX Sotir ("Savior") (142–80 B.C.E.). His reign began in 116 B.C.E., which dates the poem's events at 109 B.C.E.

BEFORE ANTIOCHUS EPIPHANIS

Antiochus IV Epiphanis ("Made Manifest") (215–164 B.C.E.) was king of Persia from 175 to 165 B.C.E. The "great fight" to which the Macedonians have returned is the continuing conflict of the Seleucid empire and its sometime Macedonian and Ptolemaic allies against Roman dominion in the Near East. Antiochus IV's brother, Selefkos IV, Philopator, murdered in 175 B.C.E., fathered a daughter, Laodice, who married Perseus, king of Macedonia, in the early 170s. Perseus fought yet another war of independence against the Romans, which ended in defeat in 168 B.C.E., at the battle of Pydna. The king's father is Antiochus III ("the Great"), who was defeated by the Romans at the battle of Magnesia, in 190 B.C.E.

JULIAN, SEEING CONTEMPT

Julian, "the Apostate" (331–363 C.E.), was born in Constantinople, where he ruled as Roman emperor from 361 to 363. At the age of twenty, he abandoned Christianity, at which he had appeared especially pious and adept, and embraced a neopaganism that was part Neoplatonist and part theurgy. He was named the Apostate to commemorate this defection. Julian was initiated as a practitioner of this religious magic, which included rain-making, miraculous healing, and animation of idols, and which was based on a theory of cosmic sympathy of the celestial and mundane orders promulgated by Maximus of Ephesus (died 370 C.E.). Julian invited Maximus into the court at Constantinople when he ascended to the imperial throne in 361, and the theurgic philosopher remained an influential counselor until Julian's death in a military campaign against the Persians in Syria in 363. Officially, Julian declared religious tolerance in Constantinople, where Christianity had been made the officially favored religion by Constantine the Great, who had renamed Byzantium after himself, in 324. In practice, Julian used his imperial authority to promote paganism and discourage Christianity, barring Christians from teaching the classics or philosophy, and launching a campaign to reinstate the worship of the pagan gods. Julian's thought and practice were austere, and earned him as much contempt as admiration from the sophisticated Byzantines. In his accomplished writings, which include the satiric *Misopogon*, an attack on what he viewed as Christian decadence in Antioch, and *Against the Gallileans*, a theological critique of Christian thought and practice, Julian promotes astringent cosmological mysticism and learned stoical morality. Cavafy was singularly antagonistic toward Julian and wrote more poems about this figure— seven—than any other, historical or mythological. The quotation that begins this poem is from a letter Julian wrote in 363 appointing Theodoros high priest of theurgic neopaganism throughout Asia. "Galatios" refers to one Arsacius, whom Julian had similarly appointed high priest, over Gaul. "Nothing in excess" was a maxim in Greek philosophy, a familiar rendering of the normative Greek standard of aesthetic moral and intellectual decorum, most rigorously elaborated by Aristotle. For two other literary treatments of Julian, see Henrik Ibsen's historical drama *The Emperor and the Gallilean* (1873) and Gore Vidal's novel *Julian* (1964).

EPITAPH OF ANTIOCHUS, KING OF KOMMAGINI
For Kommagini, see the note for "Melancholy of Jason Kleander; Poet in Kommagini; 595 A.D." For Antiochus, see the note for "Before Antiochus Epiphanis."

THEATER OF SIDON (400 A.D.)
See the note for "Young Men of Sidon (400 A.D.)."

JULIAN IN NICOMEDIA
See the note for "Julian, Seeing Contempt." Nicomedia, a port city, was the capital of Bithynia, a northwestern territory in Asia Minor stretching from the peninsula of Chalcedon into northeastern Greece. Chrysanthios and Maximus, Neoplatonists tutored in the philosophic tradition established by Iamblichos (245–325 C.E.) in Syria, were Julian's teachers in

Nicomedia. Gallos, Julian's half brother, had been named emperor in 350 by his and Julian's cousin Konstantios II. Konstantios was a devout Christian, and Gallos a nominal one; hence the "uneasiness" and "suspicions" Julian is said to be arousing in this poem by insufficiently concealing his paganism under the cloak of reverent Christian worship and study. Gallos was executed by his uncle in 354, and Julian was appointed as the imperial successor, a rank he did not actually take on until 361. Mardonios was Julian's tutor from childhood. "Liturgical reader" might also be translated as "chanter," a role of great significance in Greek Orthodox worship. The "chanter," "psalti" in Greek, chants the hymns and psalms and the epistle reading, a substantial portion of the Orthodox liturgy.

31 B.C. IN ALEXANDRIA
The false victory of Antony referred to here is his and Cleopatra's final defeat at the hands of Octavius at the naval battle of Actium in 31 B.C.E.

JOHN KANTAKUZINOS TRIUMPHS
John Kantakuzinos reigned as Byzantine emperor, together with his son-in-law John Palaiologos, from 1347 to 1354. Lord Andronikos is Andronicos II, emperor from 1328 to 1341, father of John Palaiologos, under whom Kantakuzinos had full sway over the governance of the empire. Upon Andronicos's death in 1341, Kantakuzinos became regent for the nine-year-old Emperor John. Anna is Anne of Savoy (hence the poem's reference to the "Franks"), wife of Andronicos and mother of John Palaiologos and his sister Irini, later Kantakuzinos's wife. From 1341 to 1347, a civil war raged in Byzantium over Kantakuzinos's regency, which Anne had tried to block by imprisoning him and confiscating much of his property. Kantakuzinos won the conflict and was crowned, together with his wife Irini, as John VI in 1347. The poem is spoken by an anonymous court intriguer who sided with the new emperor's enemy, Anna, and is now fearful of the repercussions. John Palaiologos forced his father-in-law to resign in 1354, upon which Kantakuzinos entered a monastery and wrote his memoirs. He died in 1383.

TEMETHOS, ANTIOCHAN; 400 A.D.
For an account of the historical masquerades in this erotic lyric à clef, see the note for "Before Antiochus Epiphanis." Samosata was the capital of Kommagini. The "137th year of the Greek kingdom" would be 175 B.C.E., dated from the origin of the Seleucid Persian dynasty by Selefkos I, Nikator ("the Victor") (312–281 B.C.E.).

OF COLORED GLASS

See the note for "John Kantakuzinos Triumphs." In 1343, Anne of Savoy, sister and political opponent of Irini, sold the Byzantine crown jewels to Venice to raise money for her plot against Kantakuzinos. They were never recovered. Hence, the glass jewels' poignancy in this poem.

ON AN ITALIAN SHORE

The "Greek spoils" referred to here were brought to Italy after the defeat of the Achaian Alliance and subsequent pillaging of Corinth in 146 B.C.E., whereupon the victorious Romans, led by the consul Mummius, carried out their normal postvictory festivities: slaughter of the men, auctioning of the women and children as slaves, and destruction of every loser's home. See the note for "Those Who Fought for the Achaian Alliance."

APOLLONIOS OF TYANA IN RHODES

See the note for "If Actually Dead."

IN A TOWNSHIP OF ASIA MINOR

For the battle of Actium, see the note for "31 B.C. in Alexandria."

PRIEST AT THE SERAPEION

The Serapeion, the temple of Serapis, an Egyptian god often identified with Isis, was built in approximately 300 B.C.E., by Ptolemy I, Sotir ("Savior"), and destroyed in 392 C.E. by the Emperor Theodosius in a persecution of the pagans.

A GRAND PROCESSION OF PRIESTS AND LAYMEN

Antioch was founded in Syria by Seleucus I in 300 B.C.E. as one of the Seleucid empire's capitals. In this poem the city's Christian history is invoked. The followers of Jesus were first called Christians here, and it was important enough as a Christian city to merit, along with Constantinople, Jerusalem, and Alexandria, a patriarchal throne in the Eastern church. Julian arrived in Antioch from Constantinople in June 362 to direct a campaign against the Persians, and lived there in a constant state of tension with the Christian population, who detested the emperor who scorned them. He died in that campaign in June 363, at which point his military commander, Jovian, was named emperor. Jovian died in February 364.

JULIAN AND THE ANTIOCHIANS

For Julian, see the note for "Julian, Seeing Contempt." Julian's *Misopogon* was a satire directed against the Antiochians for their resistance to his paganism. Konstantios is Konstantios II, Julian's cousin and his predecessor as emperor. Konstantios was a devout Christian, much involved in the struggle to achieve doctrinal unity in the Eastern church. For Antioch, see the note for "A Grand Procession of Priests and Laymen."

ANNA DALASSINI

Anna Dalassini was the mother of Alexius I Komninos, who reigned as Byzantine emperor from 1081 to 1118. In her *Alexiad*, book 3, chapter 6, Anna Komnina, daughter of Alexius, cited the decree issued by her father, which Cavafy excerpts to end this poem. The decree not only honored Anna's grandmother, but created Dalassini regent of the empire during Alexius's absence in 1081.

GREEK FROM ANCIENT TIMES

For Antioch, see the note for "A Grand Procession of Priests and Laymen." Io, daughter of the river deity Inachos, a priestess of Hera at Argos, was changed into a heifer by the amorous husband of that goddess, Zeus. Hera harassed the transformed votary with gadflies all the way to Egypt and to Syria, where the white girl-cow gave up the ghost. Her brothers built Iopolis (a precursor of the Ione mentioned here) on the site to honor her. Iopolis was renamed Antioch by Seleucus in 300 B.C.E. See Ovid's *Metamorphoses*, book 1, verse 748.

YOU DIDN'T UNDERSTAND

For Julian, see the note for "Julian, Seeing Contempt." Julian's quip was made in a letter (letter 81 in the Loeb Classics *Julian*, vol. 3, p. 286) to Basil of Caesarea (330–379 C.E.), a classically educated father of the Christian Church, famous for his formation of monastic norms in the Eastern Church, and for his letter "An Address to Young Men," which explained how classical literature was to be interpreted as edification for Christian scholars. The response, presumably, came from Basil.

IN SPARTA

In 228 B.C.E., Kleomenis III, king of Sparta from 235 to 222 B.C.E., sought the aid of his patron, Ptolemy III, in a war against the Achaian League, which he won in 227. Ptolemy's terms were that Kratisikleia,

Kleomenis's mother, be sent, together with his children, to Alexandria as hostages. Eventually, Kleomenis failed in his attempts to enlarge Spartan holdings in the Peloponnese and fled to Ptolemy III himself in 222. Ptolemy III died in 221, and his successor, Ptolemy IV, imprisoned Kleomenis, who killed himself in 220. His body was flayed and subsequently crucified. The Lagid family, from whom the Ptolemies were descended, were lowborn Macedonian, and from the Spartan perspective, their dynastic order was contemptibly nouveau. The source is Plutarch's *Life of Agis and Cleomenis*, chapter 22.

KIMON, SON OF LEARCHOS, AGE 22, STUDENT OF GREEK LITERATURE (IN KYRINI)

Kyrini was Cyrene, present-day Shahat in Libya, the major Greek colony in Africa. Situated eleven miles from the Mediterranean, it was an important center of trade, learning, and literature. Callimachos, active from 280 to 245 B.C.E., the preeminent Hellenistic poet and scholar, author of more than eight hundred books of poetry and prose, was born in Kyrini—as were the fifth-century–B.C.E. philosopher Aristippos, an associate of Socrates; the philosopher Carneades (214–128 B.C.E.), a founder of the New Skeptical Academy in Athens; and Eratosthenes (285–194 B.C.E.), a scholar who was appointed head of the library at Alexandria in 245 B.C.E.

ON THE MARCH TO SINOPI

Mithridates is Mithradates V, Euergetes ("Benefactor"), from 152 to 120 B.C.E. king of Pontus, a northern region of Asia Minor that included the southern coastal area of the Black Sea and extended southward to Cappadocia. The capital of Pontus was Sinopi. Mithradates adeptly extended his territorial boundaries; for his help to the Romans in their campaign against Carthage, he received Phrygia, the central plain of Anatolia, present-day Turkey. He gained influence over Cappadocia by marrying his daughter to the king of that region, and friendly presence to the Seleucid empire by marrying a Seleucid princess himself. This conventional expansionism proved conventionally disastrous, as his wife was implicated in the plot that led to his assassination in Sinopi in 120 B.C.E. The tale of silent communication by which the soothsayer admonishes Mithridates' messenger refers to an earlier assassination attempt planned by Mithridates I against his son Mithridates II in 301 B.C.E. Dimitrios, later Dimitrios I of Macedonia (see the note for "King Dimitrios"), who had been sworn to silence about the murder plot against his friend, revealed it to Mithridates by tracing in the ground the message which ends this poem: *Flee Mithridates*.

ALEXANDROS IANNAIOS, AND ALEXANDRA

Alexander Janneus ruled Judea from 103 to 76 B.C.E. The work begun by Judas Maccabaios and his four celebrated brothers (John, Jonathan, Simon, and Eleazar) was the liberation of Judea from the Seleucid empire, and especially of Jerusalem and the temple therein from the hellenizing forces of that empire in 142 B.C.E. Judas and his brothers were the sons of Matthatias, whose descendants ruled Israel, in politic collaboration with the Seleucids, as high priests and kings of the Asmonaean dynasty, until Pompey took Jerusalem from them in 63 B.C.E. For more on the Asmonaean dynasty, see the note for "Aristovoulos." Alexander Janneus was an Asmonaean through the line of Simon, and was famous for minting coins with monarchical assertions written in Greek, Aramaic, and Hebrew, as well as for his tyranny, which led to his executing eight hundred Judeans to please his concubines, after which he died, drunk, in 76 B.C.E. Asmonaean power over Judea passed to the Romans soon after Alexander's successor, Alexandra, died in 67 B.C.E.

COME, O KING OF THE LACEDAIMONIANS

See the note for "In Sparta." The scene and quotation are from Plutarch's *Life of Agis and Cleomenis*, chapter 28. Sometime after 221 B.C.E., under the reign of Ptolemy IV, who took the throne after her son's protector Ptolemy III died, Kratisikleia was executed.

THEY MIGHT HAVE BOTHERED

The protagonist of this poem is trying to find a place in government service in Syria sometime between 125 and 123 B.C.E. Kagergetis, Greek for "Malefactor," was the sarcastic reversal of the surname Euergetes, "Benefactor," of Ptolemy VIII, who ruled in Egypt from 145 to 116 B.C.E. Kagergetis was also called Physcon, meaning "bloated belly or bladder." Greeks in the Seleucid dynasty called him this because of his extravagant cruelty, especially to intellectuals, and his hedonistic self-indulgence. Zabinas was an alternate and disparaging name for Alexander, the rumored son of Alexander Valas. The father stole Syria's throne from Dimitrios Sotir, whom he killed in 150 B.C.E. (See the notes for "The Favor of Alexander Valas" and "Of Dimitrios Sotir [162–150 B.C.]".) Aided by Ptolemy VIII, the son stole the throne of Syria from Dimitrios II, Nicator, in 125 B.C.E., and held it until 123 B.C.E., when he was killed by Antiochus VIII, Grypos ("Hooknosed"). Grypos reigned from 123 B.C.E. until his assassination in 96 B.C.E. Hyrkanos is John Hyrkanos, son of Simon Maccabaeus. (See the note for "Alexandros Iannaios, and Alexandra.") He reigned as king of Judea from 134 to 104 B.C.E., and was much involved, as a profiting and amused spectator, with the passing of the Syrian throne from murdered to murderer. To be aided in Syria by Hyrkanos, whom, it should be noted, he does not disparage, our hero would have to travel to Jerusalem; hence his words "I'm off immediately..."

IN THE YEAR 200 B.C.

During his campaigns in Asia, Alexander of Macedonia would bring booty from conquered kingdoms to Athens. The inscription with which he sealed the plunder, whose words Cavafy uses to open this poem, can be found in Plutarch's *Life of Alexander the Great*: "Alexander the son of Philip and the Grecians, excepting the Lacedaemonians, have won this spoile upon the barbarous Asians." The Lacedaemonians are the Spartans, who would not take part in Alexander's hellenizing expansion into Asia. Granikos was the site of a victorious battle against the Persians at the river of that name in 334 B.C.E.; likewise, Issus in 333 B.C.E., and Arbela in 331 B.C.E. For six hundred years after Alexander's conquest, Greek was the lingua franca of the Alexandrians, Seleucians, the Antiochians, and the Ptolemies, and hence of Judaic, Christian, and pagan civilization—religious, intellectual, artistic, economic, and political—throughout the southern, eastern, and northern Mediterranean world. Bactria was a huge region of central Asia, bordered by the Oxus River on the north and the Hindu Kush on the south, roughly the area between present-day Afghanistan to the north and Uzbekistan to the south. The main Bactrian satrapy was seated in Ali Khanoum, a city on the Oxus River, which Alexander renamed Alexandria Oxiana after fighting fiercely to win it. The Seleucian monarchs kept Bactria Hellenic until 130 B.C.E., when invaders took the region from Heliocles and subsequently eliminated all Greek presence from the region. The poem is spoken by a cosmopolitan Greek of the Asian Alexandrian empire in response to reading Alexander's inscription in 200 B.C.E. The speaker's vaunting is ironically offset by the titular date: Within three years, at the battle of Cynoscephalae, and within ten, at the battle of Magnesia, Rome would defeat the last Macedonian Philip and Antiochus III, respectively, and so end the "magnificent" new Greek world the speaker extols here.

IN THE DISTRICTS SURROUNDING ANTIOCH

Babylas was Bishop of Antioch from 237 to 250 C.E. Martyred, he was buried in the vicinity of Apollo's temple there, in a grove at Daphni, a rural area five miles south of Antioch whose natural springs supplied the city's drinking water. Apollo's priests, who had been appointed at Daphni by

Syria's kings since Seleucus I, circa 300 B.C.E., abandoned the temple they now regarded as desecrated, upon which the Christians built a church to honor their martyr. Sometime after his arrival in Antioch to conduct a military campaign against the Persians, Julian commanded that the offending corpse be exhumed and the church razed. On November 22, 362, five months after Julian's arrival in the city, the body was exhumed, and, on the same night, the temple of Apollo was destroyed by a fire attributed, but never conclusively, to vengeful Christians.

HIDDEN POEMS: 1884–1923

DÜNYA GÜZELI
The title is Turkish for "the most beautiful of all the beautiful women." The expostulation "Prophet" refers to Mohammed. Istanbul is the modern Turkish name for Constantinople.

NICHORI
Nichori was a Greek summer resort area on the European shore of the Bosporus Strait, not far from Constantinople. Its ancient name was Neapolis, "New City." Cavafy's maternal grandfather, George Fotiades, had a villa there, which the poet, aged twenty through twenty-two, visited with his family from early 1883 until October 1885.

STEPHANOS SKILITSIS
Stephanos Skilitsis, a younger friend of Cavafy's, died in Alexandria on April 8, 1886, at the age of nineteen.

CORRESPONDENCE ACCORDING TO BAUDELAIRE
Charles Baudelaire, French symbolist poet, was born in Paris in 1821 and died there in 1867. Stanzas 2 through 5 of this poem are a loose translation of Baudelaire's "Correspondences," the fourth poem in the first section, "Spleen et Ideal," of Fleurs du mal ("The Flowers of Evil"), published in 1857.

"NOUS N'OSONS PLUS CHANTER LES ROSES"
The title ("We No Longer Dare Sing of the Roses") is taken from René-François-Armand's (pseudonym Sully Prudhomme) poem "Printemps oublié," "Forgotten Spring." Sully Prudhomme (1829–1907), a leader of the Parnassian school, which stressed impersonality in poetry, received the first Nobel Prize in literature in 1901.

THE MIMIAMBI OF HERODAS

Herodas was a satirical Greek poet who flourished in the third century B.C.E. "Mimiambi" are comic sketches of low events and people, written in the satiric meter of classical poetry, the iambic. In 1891, seven of these mimiambi were discovered in a papyrus. Cavafy refers to numbers 1, 2, 4, and 7 in this poem.

THE HOSPITALITY OF LAGIDES

Lagides is the family name of the Ptolemaic dynasty, derived from the first Ptolemy, Sotir I's, descent from the lowborn Macedonian Lagus. Ptolemy Philopator ("Father-loving") reigned as king of Egypt from 221 to 205 B.C.E. The epithet is an ironic reference to his supposed involvement in his father's murder in 221 B.C.E. Medon was a common Greek name in this period and is fictitious here. A mina was worth one hundred drachmas, an extremely small sum.

PRIAM'S SPEEDING FORTH AT NIGHT

This poem recasts events narrated from lines 143 to 457 in book 24 of Homer's *Iliad*.

EPITAPH

The Ganges is the holiest river of India; Samos is a Greek island in the Aegean, off the coast of Asia Minor.

A DISPLEASED VIEWER

Menander (334–292 B.C.E.) was the leading Greek playwright of New Comedy. He is famous for his mastery of plot, especially for the balance of variation and suspense by which he gave an elegance to the low domestic situations, usually amorous complications, which he treated. Gavrentios is a satiric invention; Terence, Publius Terentius Afer (183–159 B.C.E.), was a Roman playwright who adapted Menander's plays to Roman tastes. The Atellan theaters refer to Atelana, a city in the Clanis valley, in Italy, for which the Atellana, a classical species of farce somewhat like the commedia dell'arte, concentrating on stock characters and situations, was named.

TO JERUSALEM

The first poem is written in "purist" Greek; the second in demotic, or common, speech. Modern Greek contains vocabulary, syntax, and grammar from all the historical phases of the language. These begin with Homer's Greek and include the New Testament "koine," or "common," form that was the lingua franca in the Hellenistic period; Byzantine variations of both;

and many variations of these, including configurations used with local dialects that jostled for official status until the creation of the "purist" language in the early nineteenth century. This form introduced "purifying" elements of classical Greek into the demotic speech as part of the nationalistic fervor that swept Greece after its liberation from the Ottoman Empire in 1821. The macaronic form that resulted amounted to a foreign tongue for most Greeks, but nonetheless became the language of official discourse, and was used in education and literature. By the end of the nineteenth century, a revolt had gathered, and the demotic was restored to some degree in literature and, eventually, in schools. Throughout the twentieth century the linguistic battle was fought out in the government, with liberal forces favoring the demotic and conservative forces favoring the purist forms. The purist form's last hurrah came with the military dictatorship that ruled Greece from 1967 to 1974, after which the demotic, currently the primary form used at most levels of Greek life, once again became preferred. Cavafy wrote entire poems in the purist form early in his career, but abandoned it for a style that is mostly demotic, with occasional touches of purist diction and syntax.

The poem narrates an appalling event from the First Crusade. On June 7, 1099, under the command of Raymond IV de Saint-Gilles, the French Crusaders began their siege of Jerusalem. This poem narrates the crusaders' awestruck piety, with a hidden irony in the comparison of them to children. This irony is compounded by the fact that on July 15, the French Roman Catholic knights were no longer weeping but sacking Jerusalem, slaughtering every Muslim in the capital and rounding up every Jew to be burned alive in the main synagogue. Afterward, the Christian warriors gathered in the Church of the Holy Sepulchre to vaunt, in unusually bloodstained prayer. These pious Europeans were referred to in the Eastern world as "the little children from the west."

IN THE HOUSE OF THE SOUL

The epigraph and poem seem heavily indebted to "La Mort de la jeunesse," "The Death of Youth," by the Belgian poet and novelist Georges Rodenbach (1855–1898).

LA JEUNESSE BLANCHE

The title, "White Youth," is from *La Jeunesse blanche*, an 1886 collection of poems by Georges Rodenbach.

DISTINGUISHING MARKS

Himerios was a Greek rhetorician (310–390 C.E.). He taught in Athens, where his pupils included Gregory of Nazianzus (329–389), and

Basil of Caesarea (330–379), who later became important church fathers in Eastern Orthodox Christianity.

Arjuna is a hero of the *Bhagavad-Gita* (*"The Song of the Blessed One"*), an interpolation in the eighth book of the *Maha-bharata* ("The Great War of Bharata"), India's Hindu epic, written in Sanskrit and completed by 600 C.E. The theme of the epic is the struggle between two brothers, Dhritarasthtra and Pandu, heads of the Kaurava and the Pandava families, for the throne of India. Arjuna is descended from the Pandava family, which prevails. Krishna, a central deity in Hinduism and an avatar of Vishnu, the supreme Preserver, appears in the *Bhagavad-Gita* as a charioteer who helps Arjuna in his struggles. In the complex ontology of the poem, Arjuna shares with Krishna an incarnation of the twinned deity Nara and Narayana, Krishna embodying Narayana and Arjuna embodying Nara. Thus, the dialogue here can be read as a psychomachia, a war within one soul. Arjuna's task in the epic is to be the disinterested but perfect warrior, and so, as the ideal king, ensure peace. The scene between Arjuna and his charioteer, Krishna, which Cavafy has drawn here, occurs at dawn on the first day of a significant battle, when Krishna preaches the *Bhagavad-Gita* to Arjuna.

SALOME

Herod Antipas, son of Herod the Great (ruler in Judea, 37–4 B.C.E.), was tetrarch over Galilee, the region of Jesus and John the Baptist, during their ministries, from 4 B.C.E. to 39 C.E. He married Herodias, his niece and the wife of his brother Philip, tetrarch over north Transjordan, while Philip was still alive. For this flagrant violation of Mosaic law, he was publicly and vituperatively opposed by John the Baptist. To quell this challenge to his rule, Herod, somewhat unwillingly and at the prompting of his wife, who worked a machination with her daughter, Salome, had John imprisoned and beheaded in 31 or 32 B.C.E. Salome later married her uncle Philip. In the Gospels she is referred to only as the daughter of Herodias.

It is Josephus, Greek historian and Jewish priest (37–c.100 C.E.), who identifies her as Salome, in *Jewish Antiquities* (93/4 C.E., book 18, chapter 5, lines 136–38). The story of the beheading is told in Matthew (14:1–12) and Mark (6:14–29). At his birthday feast, inflamed by his stepdaughter's dancing, Herod promised the girl anything she asked for. At her mother's prompting she asked for John's head on a charger. Unable to dissuade her, Herod had John beheaded. His head was brought to Salome, who brought it to her mother. Cavafy found the variant of the Salome story he presents in this poem in *Le Journal* (no. 1232, 11 Fev. 1896), where it is cited as derived from an ancient Nubian gospel.

CHALDAIC IMAGE

Chaldaea was a region of ancient Babylonia. In the Mesopotamian creation myth, Ea was the earthly god of wisdom. Apsu, a goddess of chaos and of sweet waters, had Mummus Tamat as her consort.

JULIAN AT THE MYSTERIES

For Julian, see the note for "Julian, Seeing Contempt." This poem relies heavily for its narrative and details on Edward Gibbon's *History of the Decline and Fall of the Roman Empire*, chapter 23.

THE CAT

Bubastis, a city on the Nile Delta, modern Tell Basta, was the capital of Egypt in the Twelfth (2000–1786 B.C.E.) and Seventeenth Dynasties (1570–c.1342 B.C.E.). Ramses was the name of three rulers in the Nineteenth (c.1342–1200 B.C.E.) and Twentieth (1200–1085 B.C.E.) Dynasties. The moralizing psychology with which the cat is presented and the closing reference to Egyptian animal deification have a touching biographical dimension. Cavafy, who wrote this poem sometime near 1897, had a pet cat from 1898 to 1908, whose death caused him great sorrow.

LOHENGRIN; SUSPICION

Cavafy's library included an Italian libretto of Wagner's opera *Lohengrin* (1846–1848). The opera is the story of a dispute over the throne of Germany and its resolution, which leaves virtue restored but innocence, the heroine Elsa's most poignantly, defeated. "Lohengrin" presents the moment in act 1 in which Telramund, uncle to Elsa of Brabant, accuses her of murdering her brother at the command of a secret lover and so disrupting the succession, which he claims now belongs to him. Elsa exculpates herself with the claim that she has dreamed of a knight who will arrive to vindicate her. Telramund challenges Elsa to produce her knight. The king's Herald summons the vindicator three times, and at the third summons, Lohengrin appears in a swan-drawn boat. Cavafy's poem has Lohengrin fail to appear and so focuses tragically on Elsa's visionary faith, a change which breaks the letter but obeys the spirit of the opera's plot.

"Suspicion" concentrates on Telramund, the antagonistic character who wrecks havoc in the opera by spreading his suspicion eventually to

Elsa. It is he "who will speak of the worst," and who in fact has been deceived about Elsa's guilt by his wife, Ortrud, who envies the beautiful and innocent girl. At the end of act 1, Lohengrin spares Telramund's life after defeating the accuser in combat and so exonerating himself of the charge that he is Elsa's murderous lover. He does love her, and they are to be married, on the condition that she never inquire into his origin or ask his name. Telramund's victory, ironically so named by Cavafy, consists in his successfully seeding enough doubt in Elsa's mind at the beginning of act 2 that she eventually asks Lohengrin his name, on their wedding night, in their bridal chamber. Lohengrin kills Telramund, who rushes into the nuptial scene at this point, and then reveals that he could have returned Elsa's brother to her through the power of the Holy Grail, which he wields, after a year, had she not doubted him. He gives Elsa three gifts, including a magic sword, which she is to give to Gottfried upon his promised return. By the end of act 2, the swan boat that brought Lohengrin to the palace in act 1 reappears, and the swan is transformed into Elsa's missing brother, Gottfried, in whose arms Elsa dies while Lohengrin is drawn back to his magic kingdom in the boat. Cavafy's interpretation enhances the opera's tragic irony of faith failing victoriously, and deemphasizes the transcendent, salvational emotion of Wagner's opera.

THE INTERVENTION OF THE GODS

Ralph Waldo Emerson (1803–1882), American poet, essayist, and philosopher, advocated a "spiritual vision" of experience that had much to do with Plotinus (204–270), the Neoplatonist philosopher, educated in Alexandria, whose thinking engages many of Cavafy's Hellenistic protagonists. The Emerson excerpt Cavafy has made the poem's first epigraph is from "Give All to Love," from *Poems* (1847). After advocating total surrender to love, the poem recommends "Keep thee to-day / Tomorrow, forever, / Free as an Arab / Of thy beloved." Emerson's final stanza, the last lines of which Cavafy has only partly cited, reads: "Though thou loved her as thyself, / As a self of purer clay, / Though her parting dims the day, / Stealing grace from all alive, / Heartily know, / When half-gods go, / The gods arrive."

Alexandre Dumas, fils (1824–1895), was a French novelist and dramatist. He treated the elite of the Second Empire and Third Republic in France with an austere moralism, which he applied to sexual topics considered taboo at the time. The play alluded to in this poem's epigraph, *L'Étrangère* (1876), takes up marital infidelity. Cavafy shifts the erotic context these excerpts establish into a tragic dimension by reference to the descent of gods from machines, the classical deus ex machina, by which deities abruptly intervene to resolve tragic plots, especially in the plays of Euripides (c.480s–407/6 B.C.E.).

KING CLAUDIUS
Claudius is the usurping, murderous, adulterous antagonist of his nephew, Hamlet, in William Shakespeare's tragedy *Hamlet* (1601).

THE NAVAL BATTLE
This poem is an imitation of the choral odes in *The Persians* (472 B.C.E.) by Aeschylus. That tragedy relates the return of Xerxes to Persia after he has failed to conquer Greece. The naval battle lamented in this poem is the battle of Salamis, which took place in September 480 B.C.E. The battle took its name from the island of Salamis, situated in the Saronic Gulf, off the coast of Athens. Defeated here, the Persians retreated to their homeland. Aeschylus himself had fought against the Persians in the battle of Marathon ten years earlier. Ecbatana was an ancient capital of Media and was conquered by Alexander in 330 B.C.E. For Susa, see the note for "The Satrapy." Persepolis, a capital of the Persian Empire, was taken by Alexander in 320 B.C.E. The repeated lamentations in lines 2, 20, and 22 are Greek transliterations of Persian cries of anguish and despair, a linguistic debt to Aeschylus.

WHEN THE WATCHMAN SAW THE LIGHT
This poem recasts the prologue to *Agamemnon* (458 B.C.E.), the first play of Aeschylus's *Oresteia* trilogy, which also includes *Choephori* and *Eumenides*. In that prologue a watchman is stationed on the roof of Agamemnon's palace, the ancestral seat of the house of Atreus (from which Agamemnon is descended), in Argos, in the southern Peloponnese. There the watchman sees the symbolic fire lit on Mount Arachnaion that announces the end of the Trojan War and the return of Agamemnon.

POSEIDONIANS
The *Deipnosophistai* (*"The Learned Banquet"*), from which the epigraph of this poem is excerpted, was composed by Athenaios, a Greek writer from Naucratis in Egypt, who flourished circa 200 B.C.E. The work is a symposium, a literary form in which wisdom is dispensed by dinner guests at a feast. The form, which was widespread through classical and Hellenistic Greek writing, is at least as old as Plato's *Symposium* (378 B.C.E.), and informs the Last Supper scenes of the New Testament, especially that of the

Gospel According to John. The form also made a unique appearance in Christian Greek literature as the *Symposium* of Methodius of Olympus (died 311 B.C.E.), who reset Plato's dialogue in an apple orchard and recast it as an all-female discourse on virginity.

Athenaios's work casts his patron, Larensis, as the Roman host of the *Deipnosophistai*, which quotes more than 10,000 lines of poetry, cites 1,250 authors, and refers to more than 1,000 plays by their title. The work, in which Galen appears, together with a Cynic philosopher, takes place over three days, during which, in addition to law, medicine, philosophy, and literature, the numerous guests discuss the variety of customs and practices observed on holidays and in social celebrations.

Poseidonia, better known by its Latin name, Paestum, was a Greek colony founded by Sybaris in 600 B.C.E. some one hundred miles southeast of Naples, near present-day Salerno. The term *sybarite*, meaning a voluptuary, or sensualist, is derived from the culture of indulgence for which the colony became legendary. Ironically, the colony was also famous for its Greek temples, the ruins of which survive to this day. In 273 B.C.E., Rome conquered the colony and renamed it Paestum. Tyrrheneans are the Greek-named Etruscans; Italiotes refers to Greeks of southern Italy.

THE END OF ANTONY

For Antony, see the note for "The God Forsakes Antony." The mistress with eastern gestures referred to here is Cleopatra.

27 JUNE 1906, 2 P.M.

On this date five Egyptians, aged twenty-two to eighty, were hanged by the British for resisting the provocative behavior of British police officers in the Egyptian town of Densouai. Cavafy concentrates exclusively here on the youngest condemned, whom he regarded as innocent, whose age he changed to seventeen, and whose name, Joseph Housein Selim, he included in the manuscript of the poem.

"THE REST I WILL TELL TO THOSE BELOW IN HADES"

The title of this poem is also the 865th line of *Ajax*, a tragedy by Sophocles (496–406 B.C.E.). Ajax delivers this line immediately before he kills himself. Proconsuls were governors or military commanders of Roman provinces, with fairly wide discretionary authority. The sympathy the poem's speaker, the proconsul, feels with the umbrageous military hero Ajax, his implicit ennobling comparison of his own private anguish to that of Ajax, and his anticipation of a liberating, vindicating future community in Hades for previously silenced wronged heroes are all cast into doubt by the sophist's reminder that worldly concerns may have vanished in the afterlife. The irony is masterfully unstable, since in Hades, as Homer depicts it, both in *The Iliad* and *The Odyssey*, the primary sources for Greek views of the soul's condition after death, heroes do little else except elegiacally review the wrongs they suffered in life. Thus, the poem dramatizes, in literary terms, the complex power relations of colonial and imperial mentalities, with the poet, a Greek intellectual professional, subversively appropriating a Roman commander's self-aggrandizing usurpation of Greek heroism.

RETURN FROM GREECE

Hermippos was a common ancient Greek name. The silent listener of the anonymous speaker may be, if he is not fictional, the grammarian Hermippos of the second century C.E., who, born a slave, gained an education and eventually wrote *Interpreting Dreams, On the Number Seven*, and *About Slaves Eminent in Learning*. His teacher was Philon of Byblos, a port city of Phoenicia, Jubayl in present-day Lebanon. Philon (70–160 C.E.) wrote a Greek history of Phoenicia that recast that culture's religion and mythology in distinctly Hellenistic terms.

EXILES

The speaker is fictional, but details of his narration, especially the dream of overthrowing Basil and the citation that the Alexandrian Christians have Roman sympathies, date the poem's events in the period after 867, the year that Basil I took the throne of Byzantium from Michael III, whom he had murdered. In that same year Basil deposed the patriarch, Photios, who had initiated hostilities with the papacy. The exiles referred to in the poem's title belong both to Photios's party and to the murdered Michael's. The poet referred to, Nonnos the Panopolitan, was an Egyptian Greek poet (c.450–470 B.C.E.), whose *Dionysiaca*, in forty-eight books, the sum of the books in Homer's *Iliad* and *Odyssey*, explicitly presents itself as an attempt to outdo Homer in narration of the divinities. Nonnos was famous for a style that matched extravagantly complex and luxuriant rhetoric to strict metrical composition. Alexandria, of course, was a center of literary theory, especially of Homeric scholarship and interpretation, from the fourth century B.C.E. to the third century B.C.E., when the methods and theories formally applied to Homer, especially allegorical ones, were adapted to the study of the Bible. There is, therefore, something anachronistic about Nonnos, for all his talent, and this adds to the aura of diminished majesty that glows everywhere in this poem.

THEOPHILOS PALAIOLOGOS

The titular protagonist of this poem was a relative of Konstantinos Palaiologos XII, emperor of Byzantium when Constantinople fell to the Turks, led by Mehmet II, on May 29, 1453. Theophilos, a scholar of mathematics and literature, died in the battle, while in command of Byzantine troops. The emperor, at whose side Theophilos died, disappeared in the battle. Legend reports that, on learning the Turks had prevailed, the scholar-soldier cried out, "I'd rather die than live." The term *kyr* is an aristocratic honorific, roughly equivalent to the English "sir," with the prestige, but not the rank, of knighthood attached. Cavafy also treats the fall of Constantinople in "Taken."

A GREAT FEAST AT THE HOME OF SOSIBIOS

The irony of this poem rests in the nature of the "cabals" and tiresome politics referred to in the last two lines. Sosibios was a councillor and minister to Ptolemy IV, Philopator. In 205 B.C.E., Sosibios and Agothocles staged a palace coup and murdered Philopator. He was succeeded by his five-year-old son, Ptolemy V, Epiphanes.

SIMEON

Libanius (314–393 C.E.) was born and died in Antioch. He was a Greek rhetorician who rose to great prominence in the intellectual, ecclesiastical, and political circles of Hellenistic and Christian Asia Minor. His students in Athens included Julian the Apostate, later emperor in Constantinople from 361 to 363; John Chrysostom (347–407), later bishop of Constantinople, Father of the Eastern Church, and Doctor of the Western Church; and Basil of Caesarea (330–379), later bishop of Caesarea. Meleager, who lived in the first century B.C.E., was a Greco-Syrian poet and philosopher, famous for his anthology *Garland*, which collected epigrams of the preceding two hundred years, and which listed their authors, with a corresponding flower, in its preface. Simeon is Saint Simeon Stylites (c.390–459 C.E.). Simeon was born on the Cilician border of Syria. In 405, at fifteen, he traveled to Antioch and then Tell 'Ada, where, at the monastery of Eusebona, between Antioch and Aleppo, he lived a solitary life. In 415, at twenty-five, he climbed a six-foot pillar, whose height he gradually increased during the next thirty-five years he lived on it, until it towered at sixty feet. Cavafy inserted a note in his copy of Edward Gibbon's history of the Roman Empire, at chapter 37, where Simeon is mentioned. Of Saint Simeon, Cavafy wrote:

This great, this wonderful saint is surely an object to be singled out in ecclesiastical history for admiration and study. He has been, perhaps, the only man who has dared to be really *alone*. . . .

The glory of Simeon filled and astounded the earth. Innumerable pilgrims crowded round his column. People came from the farthest West and from the farthest East, from Britain and from India, to gaze at the unique sight—on this candle of faith (such is the magnificent language of the historian Theodoret) set up and lit on a lofty chandelier.

The speaker and Mebis are fictional literary sorts, probably Antiochans. The date is 450, nine years before Simeon's death. The speaker recovers from his spiritual disruption enough by the poem's end to make a punning return to his academic, critical wits. The Greek for Lamon, with a gamma appended, "glamon," means "mucus-clouded eyes," or "blind." A Greek proverb holds that "in the cities of the blind, glamon, [blind eyes] reign." The speaker's categorical denigration of Syria's literature, learning, and aesthetics, inferred by his naming her chief poet "Lamon," ironically puts a premium poetic, intellectual, and aesthetic value on the spiritual isolation of Simeon, one fixed on God as the supreme object of vision.

COINS

The monarchs adorning the coins described in these poems were all Greco-Indian kings of Bactria, an ancient region whose modern borders are Uzbekistan, to the north, and Pakistan, to the south. Eboukratintaza is Eucratides I (c.170–145 B.C.E.). Eucratides chronicled his career in commemorative coins, some of which bore portraits of his parents, and in rectangular, commercial coins stamped with Greek and Indian inscriptions. He was assassinated in 145 B.C.E. Strataga is Strato I, son of Menander, who reigned jointly with his mother, Agathocleia, from 130 to 75 B.C.E. Menantraza is Menander Soter, king circa 150 to 130 B.C.E. Considered the greatest Greco-Indian monarch, he spread Greek rule farther into India than any other ruler, as far as Patna, in the valley of the Ganges. For this he earned the epithet "he conquered more nations even than Alexander." The only Greco-Indian king remembered in Indian sources, Menander adopted Buddhism, promulgated the dispersal of Buddha's image throughout architecture and statuary, and issued coins that skillfully merged Greek and Indian imagery. Eramaiaza is Ermaios, the last Greco-Indian king, who reigned from 75 to 30 B.C.E.

The mountain rebels were the Klephts, guerilla fighters during the war against the Ottomans that led to Greece's independence in 1821. Constantinople fell to Mehmet II, leader of the Turks, on May 29, 1453. The songs commemorating that disaster that Cavafy refers to come from the collection *Popular Romaic Songs* (compiled by Arnold Passow, 1860). Byzantium was renamed "New Rome" as well as "Constantinople" by Constantine the Great when he made it the seat of his imperial rule of the Eastern Empire in 324 C.E. "New Rome" survives today as part of the Eastern Orthodox patriarch's official title—Archbishop of Constantinople and New Rome. The Christian Hellenistic civilization centered in the city was referred to throughout the Middle Ages, and far into the nineteenth and early twentieth centuries, as *Romania* by Greeks, who adopted the adjective *Roman* to competitively identify with their Western imperial counterparts. The phrase translated as "Imperial Greece" in this poem's last line is Romania in the Greek.

Saloniki, modern Thessalonika, was both a city and a kingdom in the Middle Ages. The kingdom, stretching from northern through central Greece, was the largest fiefdom of the Byzantine Empire, and the city was considered the second city of the realm. On March 26, 1430, while it was under Venetian rule, Thessalonika fell to the Ottomans, led by Murad, who pillaged the city for three days, murdering the men, looting the churches, and gathering up the women and children to sell them into slavery. Hence, the line repeated in stanza 2, "They've taken the City, they've taken her; they've taken Saloniki," alludes both to the 1430 sacking of Saloniki and to the 1453 sacking of Constantinople, commonly referred to as "the city," to magnify that disaster. The sense is that the sacking of Constantinople began with the capture of Saloniki, and that the sacking of Saloniki was finally finished when Constantinople fell.

Trebizond, in northeast Asia Minor, called an empire, was a Greek state that arose after the armies of the Fourth Crusade overthrew the Byzantine Empire in 1204. When the Byzantine Empire was restored in 1261, Trebizond, founded by the Comnenus brothers, David and Alexius I (the latter Byzantine emperor, 1081–1118), remained independent. It passed from Turkish to Mongol dominion variously until it was finally conquered by the Ottomans in 1461, eight years after the fall of Constantinople. An extremely cosmopolitan civilization, a trade route to the Far East for Asia Minor, and to the Middle East and Europe for Russia, Trebizond continued, after the conquest, to maintain a strong sense of its civilization as Hellenistic and Christian.

REJECTED POEMS: 1886–1898

WORD AND SILENCE

Cavafy transliterated an Arabic proverb into Greek for the epigraph to this poem, and I have followed his example by transliterating his Greek rendition of Arabic into an English one. His translation of the proverb in the poem's first line, "Silence is golden and the word silver," is loose. Translated more literally, the proverb reads: "If speaking out is made of silver, silence is made of gold." Thematically, the epigraph stands as an instance of the prohibition in Judaism and Islam of any representation of God, a prohibition which often holds language to be some species of graven image. Cavafy denigrates that prohibition in favor of the Christian worship of the incarnate God made flesh in Jesus. As second person of the Trinity, Jesus is the divine word, the Logos. The incarnation occurred in and through the power of this Logos, and it is through this divine word that the deifying restoration of man's divine image, the end of the incarnation in Eastern Orthodox Christianity, will occur. The theological ideas in this poem allow for the humanistic and erotic stance toward experience it expresses, a stance that Cavafy would elaborate extensively in his later work.

SAM EL NESIM

Arabic for "breath of gentle breeze," Sam el Nesim is a secular Arabic holiday, originally an ancient harvest feast, that is celebrated on Easter Monday in Egypt. This is Cavafy's only poem about contemporary Egyptian culture and the only one that names modern locales in Alexandria. The word translated as Egypt in this poem is "Misiri" in Greek, in turn, a transliteration of the Arabic for Egypt, "Misr." Khambari is a poor district in Alexandria; Mahmoudiya is a canal at the edge of Alexandria; Mex is one of the city's beaches; Muharram Bey is a formerly posh Alexandrian neighborhood; and Ramleh encompasses most of Alexandria, except its commercial center. Ptah is an ancient Egyptian god, worshiped as creator of the world and patron of the arts.

TIMOLAOS THE SYRACUSAN

The titular protagonist of this poem is fictional. His name is Greek, meaning "reverence for the people." Syracuse, on the eastern coast of Sicily, was founded as a Greek colony by the Corinthians in 734 B.C.E., and remained one until Rome colonized it in 21 B.C.E. Neapolis is the Greek for Naples, meaning the "New Town"; together with Marseilles, Tarentum,

Reggio, and Agrigento, it was part of Greece's colonial expansion throughout the classical period into southern Italy. Hesperia, from the Greek for "setting sun," was the Greek name for Italy and the Roman name for Spain. Ecbatana was the capital of Media, and the site of Persian monarchical residences. Nineveh, the Assyrian city of Ninua, on the east bank of the Tigris, near present-day Mobul, was the capital city of the Assyrian Empire in the seventh century B.C.E. Samos, an Aegean island off the coast of Turkey, was famous in classical times for its wine.

ATHENA'S VOTE

This poem is derived loosely from Aeschylus's *Eumenides*, the second play in his trilogy, Oresteia. In *Eumenides*, at Orestes' trial before the Areopagus for the murder of his mother, Klytemnestra, Athena votes to acquit him of blood guilt, and establishes justice by state-authorized trial as a replacement for justice by cultic vengeance law. Metis, an Oceanid, is the classical Greek personification of Intelligence. Hesiod's *Theogony* (ll. 886–900) has Zeus swallow Metis, his first wife, while she is pregnant, knowing she will bear Athena, and fearing she would bear another child who would rule the universe. Soon after this gourmandizing, Zeus has his head examined and opened, from which Athena springs forth, fully grown and armed for battle.

OEDIPUS

Gustave Moreau, French symbolist painter (1826–1898), lived mostly in Paris. An admirer of Delacroix, he was also the teacher of Matisse. His *Oedipus and the Sphinx* was painted in 1864.

A LOVE

This poem is derived from the Scottish ballad "Auld Robin Gray," written in 1771 by Anne Lindsay, Lady Barnard (1750–1825). The same poem inspired Tennyson's "Enoch Arden" (1864). Cavafy had read Tennyson and translated his "Ulysses," and he cited that poem as a source for his own "A Second Odyssey."

THE DEATH OF THE EMPEROR TACITUS

Marcus Claudius Tacitus was a seventy-five-year-old senator when, eight months after the murder of Emperor Aurelian, he was chosen by the Senate as Rome's emperor in 275 C.E. Old as he was, he moved east against the Goths in Asia Minor, but alienated the army. Cavafy has him die of the war's hardships; most sources agree he was killed by his own troops in Tyana, in Cappadocia, in April 276. Campania is in central western Italy.

THE FOOTSTEPS OF THE EUMENIDES
See the note for "The Footsteps."

THE TEARS OF THE SISTERS OF PHAETON
Phaeton was the son of Apollo and the Oceanid Clymene. He was beautiful enough to have been beloved by Aphrodite. Therefore impressed with himself, Phaeton was piqued, one day, when Ephasus, the son of Io, told him his pride was vanity, since he was not Apollo's son. Phaeton made his way to his father's sun palace, and elicited, as proof of his paternity, an unconditional promise from Apollo. With the boon in hand, Phaeton asked to drive the chariot of the sun, and the reluctant Apollo agreed, giving him strict and explicit instructions for the journey. In his sky-borne enthusiasm, Phaeton forgot them, and Zeus hurled him from the sky with a thunderbolt into the River Eridanus to prevent a conflagration on earth. His sisters, the Heliades—Merope, Helia, Phoebe, Aetheria, and Lampetia—rescued his body, buried it, and wept into the river, grieving so piteously that the gods turned them into poplars and their tears into amber. See Ovid's *Metamorphoses*, book 2, verse 340. The Eridanus was often described in classical sources as a rich source of amber.

HORACE IN ATHENS
A *hetaera*, Attic Greek for "companion," was a polite term for a woman who was recompensed for sexual favors. Hetaerai were distinguished from *porne*, "women for hire," who were working prostitutes allowed to establish themselves as entrepreneurs, much like Shaw's Mrs. Warren in *Mrs. Warren's Profession*. Hetaerai were presented in Greek literature, especially in the "New Comedy," as learned, beautiful sirens who posed infatuating dangers to idealistic, inexperienced young men, as well as to otherwise hardened seniors. Attic was the Greek dialect of Athens, used by Plato, Aristotle, and the tragedians. Horace (Quintus Horatius Flaccus), the Roman poet, lived from 65 B.C.E. to 8 B.C.E. Horace spent some part of his early manhood in Athens. After Virgil, Horace is the most famous, admired, and influential of the Latin poets.

THE TARANTIANS DIVERT THEMSELVES
Tarentum was a Greek colony in southeast Italy first established by Spartans in the eighth century B.C.E. In the first half of the fifth century B.C.E., it became home of the Italiote league, an alliance of the Greek cities in southern Italy. After an unsuccessful war with Rome, in which Pyrrhus led the Tarentian army, the colony became an ally of Rome's, in 270 B.C.E. Throughout its changing relationship with Rome, Tarentum remained Greek in language, thought, and culture.

Publication Acknowledgments

The following translations have appeared previously in the anthology and journals cited below.

"A Second Odyssey," "Athena's Vote," "Oedipus," and "The Horses of Achilles," in *Gods and Mortals: Modern Poems on Classical Myths*, edited by Nina Kossman, Oxford University Press, 2001

"Horace in Athens," *Persephone*, Fall 2000
"Morning Sea," "Candles," "In the Dull and Gloomy Village," "The Windows," *Metre*, No. 6, Summer 1999
"At the Entrance to the Café," "Ionic," *Persephone*, Vol. 4,
"In the Evening," "That They Might Appear—," *Parnassus*, Vol. 24, No. 1
"The Tobacco Shop Window," "Since Nine O'Clock—," "Remember, Body...," *Agni* 48
"They Might Have Bothered," "To Abide," *The American Scholar*, Summer 1998
"One Night," "When the Watchman Saw the Light," *The Greensboro Review*, Summer 1998
"The Ides of March," "The Satrapy," *DoubleTake*, Spring 1998
"In the Wineshops—," "Before Time Could Change Them," "The Bandaged Shoulder," *The Boston Phoenix*, January 1998

"I Went," "Desires," *Persephone*, Fall 1997
"Before the House," "In the Street," "Chandelier," *Agni Review*, Spring 1997
"Myris: Alexandria, 340 A.D.," "Trojans," *Persephone*, Spring 1995
"The God Forsakes Antony," "The Horses of Achilles," *Persephone*, Fall 1995
"As Long as You Can," "Waiting for the Barbarians," *Agni Review*, Fall 1990

889.132   Cavafy, Constantine,
CAV   1863-1933.

         Before time could
         change them.

$28.00

DATE			